'*He who would go to sea for amusement*
would go to hell for pleasure'

ANON

ISLAND RACE

AN IMPROBABLE VOYAGE ROUND
THE COAST OF BRITAIN

JOHN McCARTHY

&

SANDI TOKSVIG

PHOTOGRAPHS BY
TOM OWEN EDMUNDS

BBC BOOKS

This book is published to accompany the BBC
television series entitled *Island Race*
produced and directed by Jeremy Mills

Published by BBC Books
an imprint of BBC Worldwide Publishing
BBC Worldwide Ltd.
Woodlands
80 Wood Lane
London W12 0TT

First published 1995
© John McCarthy, Sandi Toksvig, Jeremy Mills 1995
The moral rights of the authors have been asserted

ISBN: 0 563 37053 X

Designed by Harry Green
Map and drawings of boat by Sandi Toksvig
Endpapers and rope, flag and running head
illustrations by Anthony Sidwell
Set in 11.5/15 point Bembo by BBC Books
Printed in Great Britain by
Cambus Litho Ltd, East Kilbride
Bound in Great Britain by
Hunter and Foulis Ltd, Edinburgh
Colour separations by
Radstock Reproductions, Midsomer Norton
Jacket printed by
Lawrence Allen Ltd, Weston-super-Mare

BIBLIOGRAPHY

The AA Illustrated Guide to Britain's Coast,
edited and designed
by The Readers Digest Association,
published by Drive Publications, 1984

The Ocean Almanac, Robert Hendrickson,
published by Hutchinson Reference, 1992

Mackerel Escabèche recipe taken from *English Seafood
Cookery* (Penguin Books) © Richard Stein

PICTURE CREDITS

BBC Books would like to thank the following for
providing photographs and for permission to reproduce
copyright material. While every effort has been made
to trace and acknowledge all copyright holders, we
would like to apologize should there have been any
errors or omissions.
All photographs taken by Tom Owen Edmunds except:
Martyn Clift pages 71, 121; E.T.W. Dennis & Sons 83;
John Dewar Cards 128 (bottom); J. Arthur Dixon 165;
Down Democrat 89 (Michael Flanagan); Alex Hansen
74, 96; Dennis Hardley Photography 99, 110; John
Hinde (UK) Ltd 12, 37, 44; Lord Tiverton Howell 202;
Images 66, 174, 203; J.T. Cards 128 (top); Leo Cards
200; S & O Mathews Photography 194; Jeremy Mills
58, 90 114; James Moss 86; Pavilion Publishing 95; J.
Salmon Ltd 78, 207, 215, 218; Sandi Toksvig 75, 81,
178; Whiteholme of Dundee 148.

FOR CLAUS, PAT AND STAN

ACKNOWLEDGEMENTS

This journey would not have been possible without the aid and affectionate support of the Tonto Television crew: Jeremy 'Driven' Mills, a.k.a. 'Moley'; Alex 'Sleepy' Hansen; Martyn 'Deep Voice' Clift; Tim 'Top Box' Slessor (whose idea the whole thing was in the first place); James 'Sea Legs' Hayes; James 'Sprog-Dodger' Moss; Sally 'Kitty' Evans; Clare 'I could join you' Baskott; and Tom 'Sexy Sailor' Owen Edmunds.

We would also like to thank Sheila Ableman, Anna Ottewill, Frank Phillips, Joanna Wiese, Harry Green, Catherine Vivian, Richard Cox, Charlotte Bowden, Ian Freer, Paul Hamann and all our families for letting us go.

The landlovers set to sea

 One morning, in the summer of 1987, my fellow hostage Brian Keenan woke me early and told me of a dream he had just had. He had been on a large boat sailing at great speed down the west coast of Ireland. The boat seemed to have a mind of its own and Brian wanted to take control but, as he said, 'I hadn't a baldy's notion what to do'. He went on: 'Then I saw this old fellow in a field – we were right next to the land, just zooming along – and I shouted out, "Hey you! Which way to Norway?" Now, Johnny, what was that all about?'

We never did establish the importance of Brian getting to Norway, but the idea of making a voyage on a sailing boat became one of our central images of escape and freedom. I had always wanted to learn to sail but knew no more than Brian so we spent many ignorant but happy hours designing the perfect boat. Yet the real power behind the fantasy was the idea of doing something positive for ourselves in uncertain circumstances. In captivity we had found within us new strengths but no outlet for them; no opportunity to develop and use these strengths creatively in our dark Lebanese dungeons. It took all our energies to hold on to our sanity. Going to sea offered the prospect of much-needed physical exercise and the chance to test ourselves emotionally and mentally with the natural environment rather than against that of man with his guns and chains. We felt sure that the confines of a small boat and the isolation of being far out at sea would offer no terrors for us after our enforced captivity; the keys to safety and home would be with us alone and in the lap of the gods.

After my release there were other priorities and I had to content myself with reading yachting magazines and day-dreaming about the type of boat I wanted to own. Ideally she would be a wooden yacht built on classic lines. However, my reading also acted as something of a deterrent; there was so much to learn. A friend of Keenan's was planning to sail around the world and invited Brian and me to go as part of his crew. Faced with this great opportunity I realized that, as well as needing a fair degree of experience before embarking on such an adventure, I didn't want to go off again so far into the unknown away from family and friends. We had

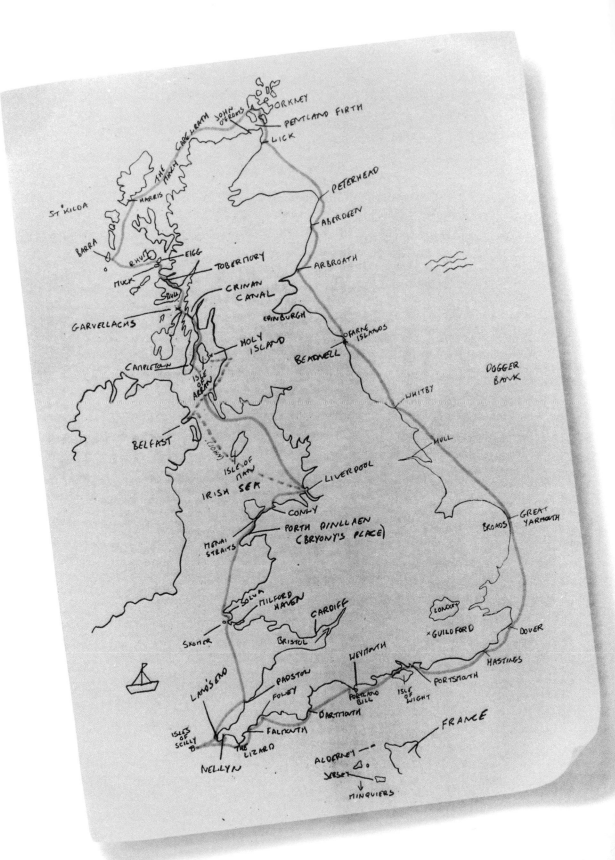

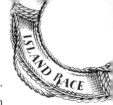

all had quite enough of that. Also I wanted to get to know my own country better. I realized that things had changed enormously during the five years I had been away. It seemed to me that the essence of the Thatcher era had been to undermine any sense of community; but had the 'greed is good' mentality banished compassion from Britain? I did not think so. My own experience had shown the huge support that people, complete strangers mostly, were ready to offer to others. I wanted to see how people were coping with life in the 1990s: how had they coped with the great and rapid changes of the past decade? Were they, as we had done in Lebanon, focusing on their immediate community and helping each other to define and achieve new goals?

It was therefore a perfect turn of fate that I should be invited to travel around Britain in a classic sailing vessel skippered by one of the country's leading yachting writers and instructors, and in the company of an old friend. I have known Sandi for years; we met in the mid-1970s when I was at university with her brother Nick. We shared a flat in London for a while before her acting and writing career really took off and I was taken off in Beirut. I am delighted to be going with her; like me, she is a novice so we will be allies in the learning process and also, famously, she has a great sense of humour, which doubtless will be helpful.

My only previous sailing experience is that I was once blown up just off the Isle of Wight in a wardrobe which had been converted into a hovercraft, but that's another story. In my nomadic childhood, Britain was the place we visited occasionally to see my maternal grandparents. It was only in the later stages of my education that I was dispatched to the British shores to receive a final academic polish. Perhaps because I don't have a youthful past of suet puddings, lemon sherbets and attempting to make things from squeezy bottles, I have always viewed British life with a slight air of the voyeur. There is so much that still seems curious to me. Any chance to dig deeper into the country I now call home is enticing, even if it does involve wearing clothing worryingly termed 'foul-weather gear'.

I have known John McCarthy half my life – he was my brother Nick's best friend at university. The two lads took pity on me as an out-of-work actress and gave me a room in their flat in Clapham. We had no money and a great time. Nick was a fledgling journalist at Worldwide Television News, I worked as an assistant chef in an old people's home and John sold advertising space in a shipping magazine. Being unable to cook, I was more likely to shorten than enrich the lives of my old folk and John wasn't much better at his job. He was far too nice to sell anything and much more likely to buy potential customers a drink than pitch a sale. He once brought a copy of the magazine home. The front cover featured a large tanker with what appeared to be a goitre condition under its bow. 'What's that?' we enquired. 'That,' he said proudly, 'is a bulbous bow.' It became his Clapham nickname.

Five years later I was working at TVS's studios in Maidstone when I got a phone call from my brother. 'They've taken Bulbous Bow,' he said. For weeks after that, while we waited for any scrap of news from Beirut, my brother did not speak. His voice had entirely left him. For the next five years there would be many hostages as we waited for John to come home.

Now I am to set sail around Britain with a hero of the nation. Bulbous Bow takes to the seas. I am absolutely confident that neither one of us has any idea of what we are letting ourselves in for …

SUPERSTITION

The journey was delayed a day so as not to start on a Friday. It is apparently unlucky to begin a voyage on a Friday, the day Christ was crucified. In the nineteenth century the British Navy thought it would step on this notion. It laid the keel of a new vessel on a Friday, named it HMS *Friday*, launched it on a Friday and set to sea on a Friday. Neither the ship nor the crew were ever heard from again.

DAY 1 Jersey

If you're going to sail round Britain the obvious place to start is Heathrow Airport. It was at the check-in this afternoon that I realized I probably wasn't quite rugged enough for this voyage. I had twenty-eight pieces of Samsonite, a 1956 AA medical kit of eye washes and triangular bandages and a box of *Teach Yourself Sailing* books. John turned up with a small rucksack over his shoulder. As it happened, most of his stuff had gone ahead by ferry but I still looked like Imelda Marcos leaving the Philippines and John merely someone popping out for a stroll.

We headed for Jersey with John and I bringing down the average age of the passengers by about forty years. The majority of people who got off the plane were very elderly blue-rinses. They were greeted warmly by the Pontins representative who kept calling out: 'It's best just to keep moving!' I think for many of them it was a life-plan rather than a travel instruction. The island is having a Good Food

Week. I've had food-poisoning twice in Jersey. I think it's a mistake to confine good food to the one week.

My geography is not exactly of the Christopher Columbus variety. My Viking ancestors tended to hit places by accident. I'd say if you wandered south of the Channel Islands you'd eventually run into France, and not a gastronomic moment too soon, but in fact the Minquiers are in the way. These small rocky outcrops, with a name which can only be said in a Peter Sellers accent, are the southernmost point of the British Isles. They're unoccupied and in dangerous waters. Yachts don't go there, so naturally they would be the best place to meet up with a 1911 wooden Bristol pilot cutter and learn to sail. Never make life too easy for yourself.

 As I was packing my gear a few days ago I watched my fellow yachtsman Robin Knox-Johnston cross the line off Ushant to complete a record round-the-world voyage in a state-of-the-art catamaran. The sea was rough, the wind looked fierce and, although smiling, Knox-Johnston and his crew-mate looked exhausted. What I was seeing on the television screen was not my idea of yachting. I felt smug knowing I had this marvellous opportunity to drift gently round Britain learning to sail, without the horrors of ocean sailing. Casually I looked up Ushant on the map. I went quite cold. Ushant is barely 20 miles further south than the Plateau des Minquiers, where a helicopter is to drop us tomorrow to begin our great journey on *Hirta*. I continued packing, but with less verve. The strange new clothes had become a warning rather than a comfort.

DAY 2 — Jersey, the Minquiers, Alderney

SHIP'S LOG: WINDS NORTH-EASTERLY FORCE 2 BECOMING 5 LATER, OCCASIONAL FOG PATCHES. SEA STATE SMOOTH.

The first thing you learn about sailing is that there's no such thing as a user-friendly tide. It always happens at unearthly hours with the intention of limiting sleep to the minimum. *Hirta* was on her way to the Minquiers and we had a very narrow time gap at high tide in which to rendezvous with her. At a time too early for roosters, John and I linked up with Angus, our helicopter pilot, at Jersey Airport.

'He looks about fourteen,' John whispered to me.

'Never mind that,' I replied. 'He's taken the door off the helicopter.'

'Give us a better view,' said John uncertainly.

'And a better chance of falling out.'

11

The weather had started out brilliantly but as we tied small bum-bags with inflatable life-jackets around our waists, the fog came in. Of course, British weather being what it is, one moment Angus had word from Air Traffic Control that we were not to take off and the next the rotors were going. Within a minute we were out and over the sea. Just. Just over the sea. The cloud was so low that Angus had decided to fly underneath it.

'I'm slightly disorientated,' he shouted. 'I hadn't expected to take off from the runway in that direction!'

John and I checked the tapes on our life-jackets.

 The seas beneath us were millpond quiet. Nevertheless I felt very nervous. I now realized I had no real idea what this voyage would require of me.

The Minquiers are just 10 miles off the Normandy coast. Ownership was long disputed between Britain and France until the International Court of Justice settled the matter in the 1950s. Having read of the battles waged over them I expected the Minquiers to demonstrate their importance physically as a massive, craggy group but I could see nothing on the horizon as we flew low over the sea. Then suddenly they appeared, like a mirage, in the early morning haze – a little collection of rocks bursting from the sea. From my bird's-eye view I had no sense of scale and the small group of houses on the largest outcrop looked somehow distorted. The impression was of something unreal, something imagined.

From the exposed helicopter pad, Sandi and I nervously edged our way around the buildings, peering through broken windows, half-expecting an axe-wielding maniac to come running at us. But there was no human here to attack us, only the birds. The thunder of the departing helicopter's

POSTCARD NUMBER 1:
The first postcard in Sandi's collection selling Britain's holiday hotspots.

engines faded and there was a moment of total silence. Then the air filled with the screams of the hundreds of seagulls. They watched beadily from the roof tops or dived, bombing us with guano which added to the mass already covering the ground, its stench filling our nostrils. After a few minutes we understood the gulls' anger; their speckled eggs were scattered under every available plant close to our feet and some were hatching. We watched, fascinated, as the shells cracked and the little feather balls struggled to get out.

⚓

SANDI The name Minquiers is from the French *minque*, meaning fish wholesaler. Extraordinary that the French can be bothered to have a whole word just for fish wholesalers, but there we are. There is a certain tragedy about the English language when you compare it with the French.

Thousands of gulls, shags and cormorants have entirely taken over the island. Bird shit is politely known as guano. We had arrived at the guano capital of the world. At the far end of the island – a good 20-second walk – the small Customs House reminds you of the seriousness with which Britain treats even its smallest outposts. Here a stone plaque proclaims the State of Jersey and warns against importing animals illegally. You wouldn't want to risk developing a colony of rabid sea birds. The miniature stone cottages appear to have sprung fully-formed from the rock. They are so small that they have a certain theme-park feel to them. Originally fishermen used them when they were out working for long periods but now they're only occupied by birds or people from Jersey in need of severe isolation therapy. It seems people do spend holidays here but I can't imagine it's in many brochures. There is nothing but birds, guano and sea.

We slipped and slid our way across the rocks to seek out the most southerly building of the UK – a single public loo. The smell of the toilet is a concentration of everything available on the island and certainly the bowl really wanted a jolly good whack with a serious scrubbing brush and a bottle of Jif. However, a large sign also helpfully points out that the nearest other alternatives are in Jersey, which is 11 miles away, and Chausey, which is 10 miles away in France.

Despite the constant noise of the birds it was, strangely, one of the most peaceful places that I have ever been to. Human beings just don't belong.

⚓

JOHN The mind and senses whirled at the beauty of the place and the security offered by such profound privacy; then whirled again to produce a ghastly mirror-image of brutal nature and the misery of isolation. A welcome and a warning. The tiny cluster of houses seemed to be an idyllic retreat capable of sudden transformation into a place of horror.

ABOVE: Hirta *moored alongside Britain's most southerly building.*

LEFT: *The inhabitants of the Minquiers watch us arrive.*

'Can you see anything?' I asked Sandi as we scanned the horizon.

'Water. Fog.' she replied helpfully.

'Great.'

We were relieved when *Hirta*'s elegant shape finally appeared. The tide was turning and, too-soon for comfort, water would surge away across the reefs and through the many channels, exposing a vast area of jagged rocks and making departure impossible. I found myself looking at the sea with a new eye as it washed over the shore. Like all evidence of man in this lilliputian landscape, set against the vastness of the sea, *Hirta* looked very frail. It was as if the sea, like an acquaintance who has never really imposed himself, was suddenly demanding all my attention – offering at once both huge rewards and dire threats. I felt a mixture of exhilaration and trepidation, wondering if we would become friends or enemies. Respect seemed the best approach to this new relationship. Respect for the elements is skipper Tom Cunliffe's byword.

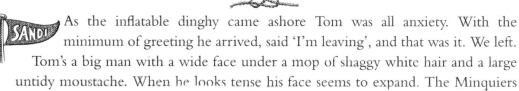

SANDI As the inflatable dinghy came ashore Tom was all anxiety. With the minimum of greeting he arrived, said 'I'm leaving', and that was it. We left.

Tom's a big man with a wide face under a mop of shaggy white hair and a large untidy moustache. When he looks tense his face seems to expand. The Minquiers made him tense.

JOHN Within no time at all Tom ferried us out to *Hirta* where his mate Pol helped us all on board. We were underway. It was obvious that Tom was relieved to start working his way out through the maze of reefs. He has what my mother would have called 'a lived-in face' which, with his whole being, seemed to lock in fierce concentration. He explained that he had never been here before and, although delighted to have made it to the Minquiers, was equally delighted to be getting away from them. One of his sailing mentors had once given him a chart for the Minquiers with 'Do not go here' writ large across it.

Tom and Pol did all the work as we left the little archipelago. Tom at the helm explained that he was navigating by 'transits' – landmarks, identified from charts for the area, to provide a safe route around the dangers hidden just below the surface. Tom and Pol were looking in all directions at once. I followed their example but could not make any useful sense of what I saw. Here was water, there was a rock.

SANDI For a good half-hour there was the kind of tension on board you normally only get in very old episodes of *The Saint*. Throughout the journey-planning Tom had always said there was only a twenty-five per cent chance that

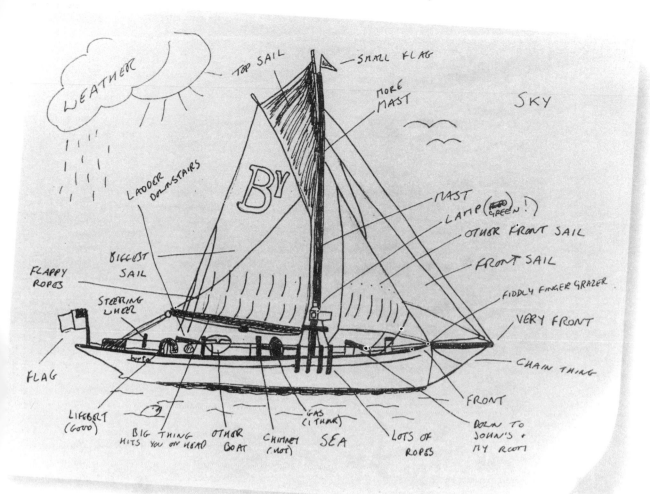

WEATHER

TOP SAIL — SMALL FLAG

MORE MAST

SKY

LADDER DOWNSTAIRS

BY

MAST

LAMP (RED GREEN!)

OTHER FRONT SAIL

FRONT SAIL

FIDDLY FINGER GRAZER

VERY FRONT

FLAPPY ROPES

BIGGEST SAIL

STEERING WHEEL

FLAG

CHAIN THING

FRONT

DOOR TO JOHN'S & MY ROOM

LIFEBOAT (GOOD)

BIG THING HITS YOU ON HEAD

OTHER BOAT

CHIMNEY (NOT)

GAS (I THINK)

SEA

LOTS OF ROPES

we'd actually get in to the Minquiers. They had been entirely fog-bound for about three-quarters of an hour coming in towards the islands. Tom had only allowed another quarter of an hour for the fog to lift before he would have aborted and abandoned the whole thing. Once we were safely away, the relief and excitement on board was tangible – we'd done it.

My nose was having a serious overload. Even after the unique aroma of the Minquiers, the first thing that strikes you when you come aboard *Hirta* is the smell of the boat. There's the strong Stockholm tar, which is a sort of pine resin that they rub on to the ropes, there's turpentine and then some special oil rubbed into the wood to make the whole thing gleam. Your nasal passages might as well have plunged straight into an episode of *The Onedin Line*.

The cinnamon-red sails lay furled on the mast ready for action. I was surprised that they were actually nylon. It seemed a little sacrilegious on the venerable vessel

ABOVE: *While John and Sandi stow absurd amounts of luggage below, skipper, Tom Cunliffe, and first mate, Pol Bergius, pilot* Hirta *away from the dangerous waters of the Minquiers.*

OPPOSITE: *The first mile of a two thousand mile journey.*

but the ropes were the proper hemp business. They were all laid out. I longed to follow each rope to find out what it did and how and why, but then I started feeling rather foolish. Like someone who'd stepped out on to the dance floor and didn't quite know what was expected of them but half-feared an offer to tango would be forthcoming. It was both thrilling and terrifying. An entirely new floating world which was completely and utterly alien to me.

JOHN Moving around the boat, even in this calm, is far more difficult than I had expected. I feel clumsy and seem to have lost all sense of rhythm. I had expected to be frustrated by my ignorance of sailing, but not by my feet. At times it feels as though I'm walking on the moon. I felt as I had when I first came home from Lebanon: even the simplest tasks were beyond me as I struggled to take in new people in new environments.

Alongside the physical dislocation my thought processes keep going out of gear. I find myself looking out across the sea thinking of what we have just done, then about concerns at home where my father is very ill, then to all I have to learn on this journey. However, these moments are massaged away when I settle in one spot and enjoy the motion of the boat.

Hirta is an engaging and reassuring yacht. Built in 1911 as a working boat, she spent her early years ferrying pilots out to bring large ships up the Bristol Channel. She was built for speed, to compete with the other pilots, and exudes a sense of power. On her first voyage from the shipyard to her home port of Barry (hence the BY on her sail) her owner picked up a pilotage job that earned him a quarter of her construction costs – a fine omen that she would be a lucky vessel.

Her interior is splendid – all fresh white paint, newly varnished wood-trim and gleaming brass – and the oil lamps in her saloon swing gently on their gimbals with the motion of the sea. There are no portholes, only a skylight, so that when below I feel strangely cocooned from the outside world as her wooden planking creaks and the water gurgles along her hull.

Going below decks involves opening the wooden doors in the open cockpit and negotiating the companionway ladder plus anyone at its foot working at the chart table. Then you have to move past the first of two heads (the nautical term for lavatory), a cabin with two berths in it opposite the galley and on into the saloon. Forward of this is the cabin, normally used by Tom and his wife Ros, which has been turned over to Sandi and me. Our cabin leads on into the fo'c'sle and another tiny head. At the moment the heads remain a constant source of confusion. There are various levers and taps (seacocks) that have to be opened, pumped and closed in a certain order to let sea water in (for flushing purposes) and then out, without flooding the boat. All the while the floor keeps moving and I try to hang on to whatever presents itself.

We stowed an excessive amount of stuff down below. *Hirta* was designed for a pilot and his mate, not two sailors, two novices and an entire film-crew. John and I each have one drawer and tried to put a few things away but we still seemed to have bags each full of stuff. We appeared to have been poured on to the boat and forgotten to say 'when'. The only way we'll ever get to lie on our bunks is to flatten our belongings with a heavy weight and sleep on them.

The kitchen, or galley, is ready for action with a neat little stove in spanking new bright gleaming silver surrounded by carrots, tomatoes, onions and potatoes just waiting to be got at. I quite longed to be at sea with some stew bubbling away. I think I have a rather romantic notion of it all. I'm sure reality will be entirely different.

JOHN Once we were well clear of the islands Tom ordered that the sails be set. *Hirta* has none of the winches that make modern yachts easier to handle. Setting the sails relies simply on human strength. Pol showed us the ropes. Sandi and I were confirmed in our belief that we really are not that fit or strong and, with our total ignorance of what to do, it's hard to imagine we will ever be more than passengers or have a full role to play on the boat.

SAILING TALK

We're not just embarking on a journey around Britain but into a whole new culture with its own language. Tom and his mate Pol speak only in jargon-jammed sentences. Tackle on the ground is 'ground tackle' but anything that is tackle that is not on the ground is 'tikle' or 'taikle' or some entirely different variation on it. The ropes pass through blocks, the inside of which are called 'shives' or 'sheaves'. One of these had come asunder, which Tom said hasn't happened in eighty-four years. This is a problem because they don't make them any more. Not surprising. No one can even say their name any more. The secret of a lot of the jargon comes down simply to vowel sounds. Don't say 'mainsail', say 'mainsul' very quickly. Same with 'topsul' and 'stasul'. (Although what 'stasul' is short for is as yet unclear.) We are separated from our new shipmates by a common language.

SANDI There are a lot of ropes and, just to help the novice along, they all do different things but look exactly the same. Pol was very clear about why we all had to put the ropes away in exactly the same fashion. He said: 'When you're sailing you should be able to reach for any rope as if you had put it away yourself. So everybody uses the same technique, which makes it much simpler and indeed much safer for night sailing.'

I had mainly planned to be asleep at night but I took his point.

JOHN There's been an exhilarating sense of detachment so far on this first day's sail. As I sit on deck writing this diary we are sailing along at a gentle 4 knots over calm water with only an occasional ship in the distance. There is peace, the easy motion of the boat and the pleasure of moving by natural power alone.

'We're glurdling along,' Tom called from the cockpit. I've never heard the word before but it seems appropriate. The passage seems to have an excellent purpose in its own right and overrides any feelings of trepidation I have had.

We passed the south-west corner of Jersey, headed north past Sark and Guernsey, and on towards Alderney – the most northern of the Channel Islands and strategically the best place to start the Channel-crossing to the mainland. As we closed on Alderney, Tom was faced with what he called a 'classic sailing dilemma'. He had to judge if, even with the engine, we could reach Braye Harbour against an increasingly strong north-east wind – which might also make the anchorage at Braye unsafe. The island certainly showed no signs of welcome. Through a thickening shroud of fog, sombre black cliffs reared up, sometimes topped by gruesome fortifications, a legacy of the German occupation in the Second World War. The occasional moan of a foghorn did little to cheer us.

Off the coast of Alderney (we think).

The Radio 4 shipping forecast brought little comfort either – the wind would stay north-easterly and increase in strength – but we pressed on.

I'd been left to steer, which seemed foolish as the seas had swelled up. 'That's a decent force 4 or 5,' said Pol. I didn't like to ask if he meant the wind or the waves. It's an immensely satisfying wheel – a huge, wooden effort with the kind of spokes you could impale mutinous crews on. Tom spins it round as if he's driving a Volkswagen. I was less confident. There seems to be acres of boat ahead of you and everyone on board standing between you and a clear view. Still, there was something of the *Before the Mast* feeling as I received my first baptism from the sea when a small spray of water swept up on to the deck and on to my back. I shall be very rugged when all this is over. I shall also have incredibly strong arms. Power-steering on *Hirta* means clinging on to the wheel and heaving with all your strength. The only problem both John and I have found is that we steer best sitting on the right-hand side of the cockpit. So we'll both end up with wildly strong left arms and right ones that are practically incapable of holding a pencil.

The *Jung Frau*, a small blue fishing boat from Alderney, came alongside. She was really bucking about in the strong north-easterly winds as fog settled rapidly round us in a great grey cloak. A long radio discussion began about tides and tactics. The deep mournful cry of the foghorn bounced out at us from the island, which had completely disappeared from view. We were sailing blind, listening to a cow in labour. Presumably if you have a house on Alderney you ought to make bloody sure that you're some way down the road from the foghorn. I wonder if the estate agents put it on their particulars?

As I took the helm from Sandi again the wind changed direction and blew harder as the visibility became ever poorer and the seas steeper. The skipper of the *Jung Frau* volunteered to lead us into the harbour through the gloom. The waters here, close to the land, are dangerous because of the rocks and some of the strongest tides in the world. Although the boat heeled over alarmingly at times, I began to appreciate, as my heart slipped back down my throat, that this was what *Hirta* was built for: sailing hard and fast in all weathers. She was not, however, designed to follow the movements of a modern motor boat. As we followed the *Jung Frau* in, I made the mistake of mimicking her movements too closely.

'Look out, we're going to gybe,' yelled Tom.

I looked around, confused. Luckily, everyone else ducked as the wind caught the mainsail, forcing the heavy boom to swing wildly above our heads, the blocks and ropes following it eagerly like some giant catapult. I was furious with myself and terrified. I could have knocked everyone overboard and did not understand why it had happened.

The *Jung Frau* seemed to be leading us away from the island but the fog was now so thick that we could only keep in touch with our ghostly guide boat by radio. Finally, the captain of the *Jung Frau* crackled over the airwaves: 'Well, you'll be all right now. You can see the harbour wall.' Clearly he was mad. I couldn't see the end of our boat. There's a lot to be said for not being in charge.

It took an hour and a half to tie up at an old lifeboat mooring and sort the gear. So much for the amateur's notion of slipping into a harbour and straight off to a salty local for a pint. As we went about our tasks John called cheerfully to me: 'Well, we're on our way. We've been to the southernmost point.'

'Yes,' said Tom. 'Only 2000 or more miles to go.'

SAILING NOTES

1 *Hirta* is a cutter because she has a single mast and two foresails. If she only had a single foresail she would be a sloop.
2 Pass green marker-buoys to starboard (that's on the right) when coming in to port (which is not necessarily on your left).
3 To coil up rope properly, hold it in your left hand and always coil it clockwise or it won't lie flat.
4 Never stand on the end of a rope that someone else is pulling.
5 If you sit at the back of the steering wheel you get the kind of grease on your jeans which never ever comes out.

JOHN Despite feeling like curling up and going to sleep we accepted an invitation for a drink at the yacht club, an unimposing modern building overlooking the quay. None of the members appears to be life-long residents but 'incomers', either retired or taking advantage of the island's relaxed tax laws. Having just arrived in foul weather I could see little charm in the place.

'Do you ever feel the need to get away?' I asked a club member. 'A break is good sometimes,' she answered, ordering another round of drinks, 'but one or two days is always enough.' She seemed sane but I was dubious. I chatted to other people but realized that, though this was the first chance to get to know a community, I was preoccupied with the new demands of living and working on a boat.

SANDI I met some typical Alderney residents – a German woman from Munich who used to run the Ski Federation of Great Britain, and an American from New York. The only English woman I spoke to left me bewildered.

'I'm married to Jim,' she announced. I nodded politely. 'Jim and I are about to go off and sail from Florida to New York.'

'That's nice,' I murmured.

'No,' she said. 'I hate sailing.'

'There are only 2400 people living on the whole of Alderney,' interrupted the German as a selling-point.

'I imagine it can be difficult living where you know absolutely everybody and everything that's going on,' I commented.

'Oh, no,' declared the American. 'We often go to parties and meet people we've never met before.'

This seemed highly unlikely as I already knew half the island and I'd only just arrived. Out of the window we could see the lifeboat being launched to collect someone who had been less fortunate in the fog.

SAILING TIPS

1 Sailing hygiene. Always wash your own mug before using.

2 The shipping forecast on Radio 4 is not the dull bit before the news.

3 Cyclonic winds are winds which can change direction at any time. These are not good winds to associate with sailing.

4 Being short is a definite advantage when the boat gybes unexpectedly.

DAY 3 Alderney

Tom's suffering from bad food-poisoning. His entire face has gone a slate-grey colour, as though he has been very badly mummified and is walking around trying to see who he can complain to about his embalming fluid leaking. He's been up all night vomiting. The doctor says we definitely won't be going anywhere today.

The locals assure me there's nowhere more beautiful than Alderney when it's sunny. Today it's grey and gloomy. John and I hot-footed it to downtown St Anne. It's a one-horse town but the rain had even kept the horse away. The cinema was closed. Probably just as well. Apparently, cinema-going in Alderney can be a bit of a trial. It seems the projector can only take half a film at a time so the entire town goes to watch, say, *Jurassic Park*, watches half and then goes across to The George for a drink while the projectionist changes the reel. As if that isn't tricky enough, the projector is constantly breaking down. Consequently the entire island has only seen half of *Indecent Proposal*.

Rush hour in St Anne, Alderney's capital.

JOHN I have never been in a situation where the weather is so important. Usually it is just a matter of wet or dry, hot or cold; now it determines danger or safety. Tomorrow we hope to head across the Channel to Falmouth, a trip that could take twenty-four hours. With the weather as it is now this is a terrifying prospect and a constant talking point.

This afternoon I went on a bizarre tour of the remnants of the German occupation of the island. I warmed to my guide, chandler Roland Neal, a large man with a full, grey beard, a very gentle nature and blue eyes that twinkle with great enthusiasm for life: one of those people who have confidence, yet are still quite shy. I mentioned the fortifications I had seen from *Hirta* and, being a keen amateur historian, Roland immediately volunteered to show me some of the long forgotten tunnels and bunkers.

The tunnels are grim; the entrance is hidden by trees in an old quarry. We scrambled up a mound of earth and rock that had fallen from the cliff and then

ducked down into the gloom. There was a foul musty smell and we sank into the thick, clinging mud of the tunnel floor. Water dripped on us as we lurched into the darkness. Here and there our torches showed up bits of railway track rusting in the mud, strands of electric cable, and blocks and planks of spongy wood that crumbled at the touch. The place was eerie, echoing the terror of its construction.

'The Germans started the tunnels in 1942 to store ammunition.' Roland's voice was hushed in the still of the tunnel. 'They blasted the rock and then drove in Russian, Polish and French slave-labourers to collect the rubble and cart it away. Thousands of people died.'

About half a mile along we found old iron bedsteads and rotting wooden shelving. There was a little spur passage going off to nowhere – and that seemed to sum it all up. The tunnels were never finished or used properly: they remain a monument to man's engineering skills but also a far greater and bleaker monument to man's cruelty.

It was a tremendous relief to return to the fresh air and get the worst of the mud off in the long wet grass outside the tunnel; there seemed a real need to be cleansed of the place. The weather had improved and a cuckoo was singing. Roland then took me for a pleasant walk along the cliffs. Normandy's Cap de la Hague was just 8 miles away, the sea looked calm and the wind light. Cows munched nonchalantly in the long grass.

'Down here, John,' Roland said unexpectedly. It was hard to see anything from the surface but once we had slithered down a hole we found ourselves in an old bunker. In the main room there were drawings done by the occupying soldiers. At the end of the complex we came to a room maybe 10 feet by 12. I felt trapped, the bare concrete walls reminding me of the cells in Beirut.

'I have to get out,' I said to Roland.

'Of course.' He guided me quickly to the surface. As if to confirm my inner turmoil the weather had changed. The wind, much stronger now, was kicking the sea way below us into a mess of crashing waves and foam. The whole situation had altered in the quarter of an hour we were underground.

Everyone I'd met so far assured me that Alderney is a paradise. 'It's a place where a beautiful young woman can walk naked through the streets with a pot of gold on her head and not get so much as a goose bump,' confided a former SAS officer to me over a drink at The Diver's pub. Some of the locals were a touch frostier about life. Two gruff gentlemen, whose advanced years were spreading across the bar, collared me.

'You people come here and make programmes about the island but you don't actually talk to the islanders.' As I had just been speaking to a fisherman who had spent all his life on the island this seemed slightly strange. It transpired that the fisherman's mother was from Guernsey, so he didn't count at all.

'So what makes a real islander?' I enquired.

'Ooh,' said one, sucking on his teeth. 'Takes at least a hundred years.' His friend nodded in agreement. This pretty much ruled out everybody in the bar apart from these two gents.

One was an undertaker and the other a builder. The undertaker freely admitted that he made money out of the wealthy people who come here to retire. 'They want burying sooner than others.'

'We may make money but we don't like them,' stated the builder baldly before turning his back on me.

Not a happy place, Alderney. Three-and-a-half miles by one-and-a-half-miles of rich people living in paradise and islanders living in temper.

I met a Norwegian sailor who, for reasons best known to himself and hopefully his girlfriend, had been sailing single-handedly from the Canary Islands to Bergen. He had been sailing along reading a book when he had been struck by a tanker from behind. It had never occurred to me that this was one of the possibilities of sailing. He'd seen a great shadow over his shoulder and then found his yacht being sucked along the side of a giant rusty tanker. There was considerable damage to his boat but the tanker sailed on.

ALDERNEY IN THE SECOND WORLD WAR

Alderney was evacuated in 1940 and the entire population moved to England. Each islander was permitted to take one suitcase. There was a gap of about two weeks between the islanders leaving and the Germans actually arriving. During that time the people of Guernsey very kindly came to Alderney in order to take some of the Alderney possessions and protect them. Oddly, they still haven't returned them. No doubt some clerical error. There was more trouble in 1945 when everyone returned. The Germans had moved furniture all over the island and it had to be redistributed. The chap in charge decided to put all the furniture together in one place with a large rope around it. Everyone gathered, he let the rope drop and everybody just grabbed their possessions. A few people got over-excited and grabbed things that were perhaps rather better than what they'd had before. For years after that the people of Alderney didn't invite their neighbours into their houses in case they spotted an heirloom which didn't actually belong to their hosts.

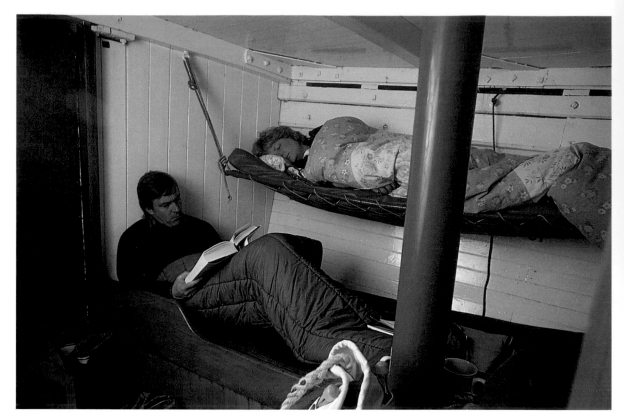

Enjoying the luxury of our state room.

JOHN I thought that I had seen enough bunkers but everyone was very excited about going to a rave being held in one so, feeling exhausted and disinclined to party, Sandi and I showed our faces at midnight. There was quite a crowd there, all ages, from children to their grandparents. The music left me cold but I couldn't help but be impressed by the organizers' enthusiasm. They believe they are creating something useful for the islanders and tourists out of the horrors of the bunker's past.

SANDI I think they should have had raves years ago. The Germans would have left in an instant.

JOHN I have felt a great sense of sadness in Alderney. There seems to be a real rift between the native islanders and the more recent arrivals, the tax-exile expatriates. The natives resent working for the rich incomers who resist new developments in order to preserve the Shangri-La that they have chosen as their place of exile. The incomers seem to view the natives as a quaint part of the scenery.

Nobody appears to like tourists. The people seem to love the place yet cannot get on with each other. The exception was Roland. I was sorry to say goodbye to my new friend.

 I've been reading a book called *Channel Island Plant Lore* by Brian Bonnard. Brian's very keen on the giant Jersey cabbage. It's a versatile plant – the lower leaves make good cattle feed, the head a delicious soup and the stem, fine walking sticks. The plant can grow so high that the head of the cabbage is 12 feet from the ground. Must be a bugger for the rabbits.

SAILING TIP
Don't forget to look over your shoulder.

Alderney to Falmouth

SHIP'S LOG: WINDS NORTH-EASTERLY FORCE 4 OR 5,
SEA STATE MODERATE, VISIBILITY GOOD.

I felt very apprehensive. It seemed likely that we were in for some strong winds and rough seas on the 130-mile passage to Falmouth, and seasickness was a real possibility during the long voyage. Tom gave us a safety briefing before we set off, going through the fire drill and man-overboard procedure.

Head to head

'I will have no sympathy for anyone foolish enough to fall overboard,' he declared. Pol reminded us: 'One hand for you and one hand for the boat.' Seemed like a good rule.

An hour out of Braye Harbour the wind picked up and the sea became very choppy. Sandi did not feel too good.

 I always thought seasickness was in the mind. I was wrong. It was in my stomach and it wanted out.

Sandi disappeared below to lie down. After a little while she was on deck again, literally flat out over the stern, being violently ill. She looked like death as she uttered her last words, 'Is Falmouth near Guildford [her home]?', before returning to the horizontal. I felt slightly guilty later on when I wolfed down some stew without any feeling of queasiness.

 Wearing enough clothes to make an avalanche seem cosy, I shivered on deck. The old saying about seasickness is that it comes in two stages. In the first you think you're going to die and in the second you're afraid you're not going to. I was reduced to undignified crawling across the decks and heaving my insides into the sea. All I could think about was that this was only the first week and there were still months to go. I managed to get downstairs and alternated sleep with vomiting into an old ice-cream container. The intrepid explorer laid low and longed for a room of her own which didn't spin.

The sea had calmed a bit as we entered some of the busiest shipping lanes in the world. *Hirta* became a small boat among very big ships on a large pond. I stood my first night-watch with Pol. As darkness fell, the compass light became the only illumination on deck. The outlines of the vessels around us vanished, leaving pinpricks of red, green and white lights. 'Red to port, green to starboard.' Pol continued his lessons through the night. 'Basic rule – always pass port to port.'

I repeated it to myself. Gradually I began to work out which way these craft were going, and to judge roughly how close they would come. Just as I had begun to feel confident, a mass of vessels appeared with extra green lights. 'Fishing boats,' announced Pol, ever cheerful. 'Pedro the Pêcheur! We'll keep an eye on him.' Concentrating on so many new things made my head spin almost as much as Sandi's.

By midnight the sky was clear and the sea beautifully calm, but it was cold. I wore thermal underwear, jeans and shirt, a jersey, a suit of warm thermal overalls and bomber-jacket topped off with a heavy suit of oilskins, gloves and a woolly hat. Irritatingly, my cigarettes were safe in my innermost pocket.

'Time for tea,' said Pol.

'Shall I make it?' I volunteered as the junior hand.

'Brillo,' he replied.

Tom slept in the quarterberth at the foot of the companionway, the camera crew on the saloon berths, the director, Jeremy, in the forecabin and Sandi, hopefully, getting some proper rest in the small central cabin piled high with camera gear. I ventured below, sure that I would wake them all as I stumbled about in the dark, but the noise of the diesel engine drowned out the sounds as I clumsily got the kettle boiling in the galley.

Back on deck, the sky was full of stars. Proudly drinking my tea, I looked up the mast to see the Plough, so clear it could have been a page from a textbook. A brilliant beam of moonlight shimmered across the black water to the port bow. I sat revelling in a new sense of detachment: I might be a million miles from anywhere. I said to myself: 'This boat is our own place, we are going our own way independent of everyone else'. Perhaps it was what all the other crews at sea felt.

I looked over the bow at the oily calm sea as it lapped at the boat. For a heart-stopping moment I thought the bow was dipping down, that we were sinking. It was as if some saintly, praying monk in dark robes had, for a split second, revealed a lethal knife, then tucked it away again and continued with his devotions. In the midst of beauty and peace I realized there was always the threat of sudden danger. The sea showed herself as a huge and mysterious animal which even at rest could turn ferocious at a second's notice. I felt like a fragile bird on the back of a rhinoceros.

Tom and Jeremy relieved us just after midnight. I think I slept for an hour, lulled by the warmth from the coal stove in the saloon and the steady rumble of the engine. Then I had to get up to relieve myself and got totally confused by the mechanics of the toilet. I gave up trying to work it but then could not relax, fearing that the boat would flood and sink. Stumbling around in the soft light from the oil lamps I disturbed Pol, who groggily showed me which levers to turn. I went back to my bunk, but still did not sleep.

Back on watch at three o'clock. Mist patches lent an eerie quality to the morning and it was comforting to see the Eddystone lighthouse blinking away off to starboard. We passed close to a fishing boat and could plainly see two men working on the deck under arc lights; the sight reminded me of walking down a street at night and seeing people watching television in their front room.

I didn't come round till about 4.30 in the morning. The first morning rays were coming in through the skylights and my tongue was just losing the taste of having been licking my jumper. I sat in the small saloon and sipped some weak tea. The paraffin lamps were lit, giving the small wooden room a slightly smoky atmosphere as coal glowed in the small stove. I could see the real beauty of the old boat. Maybe I'd make it after all.

CURRENT THOUGHTS ON SAILING
Life-jackets were a good invention.

DAY 5

Somewhere in the English Channel

By a quarter past eight it felt as if we'd been up all day. John had only managed about an hour's sleep and was looking extremely tired. Everyone had been on three-hour watches through the night but I, of course, had been missed out. The only thing I would have been able to watch was the exact state of the sea at close quarters.

A pigeon landed on the deck. It circled the boat a couple of times and then landed under the shrouds on the starboard side. It was beautiful. Not your city pigeon but a rather sleek-looking racing fellow who promptly fell asleep. The poor thing must have been exhausted because it seemed to be happily sitting there, and we were contemplating giving it a bit of bread, when it suddenly fell over the side. It had obviously fallen asleep and just slipped off. We did see it sit up in the water but Tom said that once they get their feathers wet, that's it. I had expected our first death on board after the bad weather. I'd just thought it was going to be me.

The wind grew stronger and we were soon sailing along at the break-neck speed of 7 or 8 knots. The sea had lost its oily calm and was dotted with white caps. *Hirta* heeled over a lot more and my heart pounded wildly when Tom and Pol left me at the helm to go below to check the charts and make breakfast.

'Do you want some tea?' piped Sandi from the companionway.

'I thought you were ill,' I snapped. Couldn't she see that I needed to concentrate on the boat? It was Pol, with his schoolboy enthusiasm, who reminded me of the thrill of being so in tune with the elements. He clapped his hands as he watched the wash run along each side of the boat and meet with a crash at the stern.

'It's as if the waves are running round us, clapping their hands to show how happy they are to see *Hirta*.'

Lighthouses are a brilliant sight. They mean land.

'Here's a word you'll like,' said John, relaxing. 'The old nautical name for the first sight of land is atterrage.'

'Atterrage,' I repeated. 'I'm in favour of atterrage.'

We saw the lighthouse on St Anthony Head, which marks the entrance to Falmouth Harbour, about 10 miles before we could touch the shore. The wind was blowing strongly and we were cracking along under full canvas. I missed the actual entrance into Falmouth as I was below deck by the chart table calling out the depth

of water shown on the echo-sounder. I didn't mind. It's bad form to go aground just as you arrive.

Falmouth was a pretty sight. On our right, just beyond the lighthouse, was the small town of St Mawes with its pretty little castle on aptly-named Castle Point. The great cliffs parading the coast seemed quintessentially English. Not that there was much time to stand and admire. There was much rushing to get the mainsail down but two ropes got tangled together as John and I frantically pulled at them. Keeping things shipshape suddenly seemed jolly sensible.

JOHN I was suddenly overcome by an intense desire to sleep. My body-clock was completely disorientated. I had no idea what time it was. We had been at sea for twenty hours.

SAILING INFO

1 An occulting lighthouse is not one where the devil turns the lights on. It's where the light is on all the time but occasionally flashes off.
2 People don't die of seasickness but some pigeons do.

DAY 6 Falmouth

SANDI Bad weather arrived overnight. We are forced to wait in Falmouth. Pretty place. From the harbour lots of brightly-coloured houses and pub signs invite you to wander the narrow streets leading up from the quayside. We got up in the early morning. The rain was still set in. John and I seemed to be on a typical British seaside holiday. Misty, grey. We headed for a chandler's, confident that better equipment would make us better sailors. We bought some rope to begin learning one or two of those knots that Boy Scouts can do blindfolded and which now seem useful. The small loo-roll holder with a captain on a bicycle dispensing the tissue will probably be less vital.

John inspected the many lengths of heavy anchor-chain available.

'What's the breaking strain on this?' he asked about a particularly solid chain.

'That would hold a 25-foot yacht,' replied the chandler.

'What do you want to know that for?' I teased.

'Oh, it's what they used on us in Beirut. Brian and I always wondered what it would actually take to snap it.'

We kidded about his kidnappers discussing breaking strain with the local Beirut sailing shop, but my stomach turned over. He seems so much the John I used to know that it is hard to imagine what he has been through.

The Bosun's Locker, Falmouth, Cornwall.

POSTCARD NUMBER 2: *Falmouth*.

DAY 7

Falmouth

JOHN The weather is not being kind. *Hirta* was pitching about so much that Tom decided to move her further upriver where she would be better protected from the wind. As we passed through Carrick Roads up into the narrow stretches of the River Fal we were confronted by an extraordinary sight – four enormous rusting cargo vessels lying at anchor, two from Panama, one from Casablanca and one from Liberia. Apparently this dumping has been going on for years. Companies can't afford to run one of these hulking vessels, but can't afford to scrap it, so they put it in mothballs up the River Fal. There are photographs from the 1930s when the river looks almost impassable, with perhaps a dozen ships ranged across the river at anchor. Two men live on board each vessel as caretakers. It's a very strange picture: these enormous, inappropriate tankers dwarfing beautiful, lush, unspoiled, low, tree-covered hills.

SANDI As we sailed past the *King Harry* chain-ferry, cars loaded up for the two-minute trip across the river. The ferry's owned by Viscount Falmouth. I like the idea of owning a ferry. One of the ferrymen once rescued a ferry-bound woman who reversed her car off the quay and into the water. For his trouble he received 'a splendid Chronometer and Barometer, mounted on a mahogany board with a suitable inscription' and later 'the Royal Humane Society's award on testimonial parchment'. I don't know what the woman got. Driving lessons, probably.

Tom found a good mooring upriver of the ships and we enjoyed fine Cornish pasties in the Smugglers' Cottage pub, the kind of thatched, 400-year-old pub that

Americans think we all live in. The D-Day invasion was launched from here. Nice spot for it. Tom taught us how to tie a bowline.

The knots have a wonderful and pleasing symmetry about them. My father told me that a lot of Viking jewellery and decoration was based on the patterns of rope knots. You could see that. Soon I shall be able to lash myself to the boat in a decorative manner.

JOBS NO ONE MENTIONED AT SCHOOL

1 Ferryman on the *King Harry* ferry.
2 Supertanker caretaker.
3 Chain-ferry owner.

THE CORRECT WAY
WITH A CORNISH PASTY

Hold the thick rib of pastry in your hand and eat the rest, then throw the rib away. The idea was for miners to be able to eat with dirty hands and not get filth in their mouths. So far the only person seen to eat this way is Tom.

DAY 8 Falmouth

SANDI Nearly a whole week and we're only in Falmouth. The map of Britain stretches for miles above our heads. The rather glamorous foul-weather gear we bought months ago, as a bit of a wheeze at the Boat Show, is our constant wardrobe. My every waking movement is accompanied by the sound of rustling nylon and ripping Velcro. I don't feel either of us is at our most attractive but we might do well at an Ann Summers party.

JOHN It is still raining much of the time but the clouds do seem to be breaking up a bit. We moved *Hirta* down to Falmouth Marina for more fuel and water. Coming out of the narrows of the Fal into Carrick Roads, I was full of excitement, eager to be moving off again. Two of Tom's old friends, Mike and Tina

OPPOSITE: *'This rope?'*

Rangecroft, came round for a drink. They run the annual Falmouth Classics, a gathering of old sailing boats from all over Europe, with races which sound more to do with who can get back to the pub first than serious competition. Sandi handed Tina a bottle of Alderney Liberation Rum to keep safe until our return to Falmouth. In exchange, they set us a challenge – to complete our circumnavigation in time to present the prizes for the main Falmouth Classics race on 6 August.

'No problem,' said Tom. 'As long as the weather favours our enterprise and we don't stop too often.'

Since the attraction of our journey is the chance to discover more about this island's people, we will have to balance our landfalls with the need for speed. For the first time we are conscious of the need to press on.

'So, Scilly Isles tomorrow!' Sandi said enthusiastically.

Tom sucked in air between his teeth. 'Don't get too excited. Haven't heard the forecast yet.'

DAY 9 — Falmouth

 The sea seemed very calm when I woke up this morning and I couldn't see any reason why we couldn't go. The weather had cleared. There were plenty of yachts bobbing about out at sea. Tom said he knew that was what everybody would think but that really the weather out there would be 'lumpy' and it was not the time to go at all. By evening we were restless.

'… the shipping forecast from the Met. Office issued at one seven double O …'
We listened intently to the radio.

'It'll do,' announced Tom. 'We'll sail on the morning tide. Half-five, I'm afraid.'
Isles of Scilly, here we come.

DAY 10 — Falmouth to Isles of Scilly

SHIP'S LOG: LIGHT, VARIABLE WINDS, SEA STATE CALM.

 Start your day the Stugeron way. I took two of these ultimate seasickness pills before I went to bed and woke up floating 6 inches off the ground. You might get seasick but you wouldn't care.

I'm too short to see the compass when I stand in the cockpit to steer. John has solved this by purloining a purple beer crate in solid plastic for me to stand on. Everyone is relieved that I can now not only see the compass but where we're going as well. Everything on the boat has a name, so the new addition has been named Catherine (as in Catherine the Crate).

Basic name index for *Hirta*: Charles – the main fender; Portia – another fender; Boris – a fender who was carried away by a Russian trawler but lives on in spirit; The Three Musketeers – the three inflatable fenders; Eric the Red – the tender; Moby – the inflatable; Mr Walker – the log; Bob Stay – the bob stay; Iron Bull and his various little brothers – the spanners; The Reverend – the engine; Sally the Seagull – the outboard. We asked Tom and Pol what the stove was called. It has no name. This worried them. Pol looked at it and commented: 'He needs a name. He looks a cheerful fellow'.

SAILING FACT
It costs sixty-seven pounds to fill *Hirta* up with petrol.

JOHN We left Falmouth under a cloudy sky. There was no motion in the still waters as they reflected the streetlamps and occasional glimmers from homes along the shore. Despite the smooth water, it is surprising the way the boat rolls along quite comfortably for a while, then suddenly lurches one way or the other. We motored past rocks with alarming names like the Wrigglers and the Manacles – a notorious area of coast which has claimed many ships.

Two men on a lobsterboat the size of a child's toy wished us a good voyage, as they passed, one of them puffing out his cheeks and blowing furiously to encourage a breeze for us. Fishing in a small boat in these dangerous waters must be a hard life.

At eight o'clock the tide changed in our favour, the ebb helping us westwards. The surface was disturbed by shoals of sprats which made a crackling noise. I was at the helm and Tom suddenly ordered, 'Hard a' port!' As the boat came round I saw fins cutting the water nearby on our starboard side. Tom told us it was a basking shark, valued for its liver oil, now something of a rarity through over-fishing. The 12-foot monster cruised around in lazy circles, presumably taking advantage of the sprats for his breakfast. Sandi got her fishing line out over the stern but did not share the shark's luck.

Minutes later a school of five or six dolphins broke the surface and played a little way off from *Hirta*. It is impossible not to be infected by the joy they show as they leap about. They promised a friendly companionable presence to counter the darker aspects of the sea.

There are so many ropes to learn; they each have their own name and they all look identical. Basically, each sail has one rope to pull it up and another rope to tighten it. The tightening rope is called the 'purchase' and the pulling rope is called the 'halyard'. The ropes for each sail all have their own names. The mainsail is put up with the throat halyard and tightened with a rope on the other side called the throat purchase. (I have trouble remembering the throat purchase so John and I have nicknamed it the Fisherman's Friend.) Because *Hirta* is a gaff rig, the mainsail is four-cornered with a peak away from the mast. This is pulled up with the peak halyard and tightened with the peak purchase, and so on for the staysail, the jib and the topsail. Further ropes control the height of the boom and the tension of the foresails, but that's probably quite enough for now.

When you look at a rope and can't remember what it does, the trick is to look aloft and see where it's running through its various blocks and to which parts of the sail it is attached. Which is fine unless we're in a high sea and Tom is shouting, at which point I vote to start the engine. It would be great if John and I could ever get to the stage of being able to hoist the mainsail on our own. By the time we set off on the long passages out to the Scottish Western Isles we will have to be able to carry out sail hoisting and lowering like proper crew if our journey is to be at all successful.

After a headland called The Lizard we pretty much said goodbye to land. Although the end of the mainland on the map is Land's End, Tom says that for sailors it's really The Lizard because it's at this point that you change your bearing and head out towards the open sea. I had been very nervous that I would have that dreadful seasickness again. Apparently there are fishermen who get it each time they go to sea. I can't imagine it. Why would you do that to yourself? However, the Stugeron starred and I actually managed to make bacon sandwiches for everyone.

John and I stood for a while at the bow.

'I had an image of freedom while I was away, of standing at the prow of an old sailing ship,' said John.

'It's nice,' I said. 'The wind in your hair, the water pounding on the wooden hull.' We stood silently for a few minutes. The water pounded, the wind blew in our hair. John sighed.

'Isn't there something we should be doing?'

'Don't think so.'

'Shall we go below and listen to some music?' he suggested. So we did. John put on a tape and we sat down for a while.

Galley slave.

'Can't hear a thing!' he finally shouted over the engine noise. I nodded. We sat for a bit longer. We went back on deck to see if anything was happening. It wasn't.

JOHN We carried on past Wolf Rock with its lighthouse. As we neared the Isles of Scilly, mid-afternoon, the sky cleared and the sun came out. In the brilliant light these low-lying islands were far more appealing than the cloud-covered cliffs of the Channel Islands. I felt sure we would enjoy this place – 'these sublime islands' as Tom called them. Some ten hours after leaving Falmouth we began to see the comforting sight of the buoys and markers which establish the safe channel from the south to St Mary's, the largest of the Scilly Isles. As we stood on the quayside we were able to look through the clear turquoise water and see the vast bottom of the boat.

SANDI When you've got no shower and fresh water is at a premium, keeping clean becomes rather a focus. I can cope with sleeping in my clothes for a while but I draw the line at not having clean pants. The launderette at St Mary's is up the road and along the beach from the harbour. It's not just a launderette. It's also a petrol station which sells coal and things for the garden. They were working overtime on baskets of laundry when I arrived. Apparently the only other laundry in the Isles of Scilly, on Tresco, was recently burnt down in a fire. This seems bizarre. I mean, there's a lot of water at a launderette.

St. Martin's, Isles of Scilly

POSTCARD NUMBER 3:
Why is this man's boat so far away from the sea?

JOHN I went on into the town to find the newsagent's. I bought a copy of *The Scillonian*, the island's biannual magazine. It's published, edited, written and sold in his own shop by Clive Mumford, a diffident, modest man with a great love of his island home. He enthusiastically endorsed my initial feeling that the Isles of Scilly (he corrected me when I called them the Scillies) and their people are very friendly, saying that there is a great sense of community and mutual support. He said that incomers are made welcome, while quietly deterred from any efforts to change the islands' lifestyle.

He looks forward with a sense of caution. A few years ago many islanders took advantage of the opportunity to buy their homes from the Duchy of Cornwall (Prince Charles's estate which owns the islands) and then sold them on to incomers,

at great profit, only to find that younger relatives could no longer afford the older houses. I got the impression that this brush with greed was seen to have backfired and would not be repeated.

With my copy of *The Scillonian* I wandered back to the beach where I stopped to take a picture of the mainland ferry, called – surprise surprise – *The Scillonian*, unloading supplies, including a couple of cars. I was conscious that someone was standing behind me and turned to find a wiry, wispily-whiskered old man standing patiently until I had taken my snap.

'Sorry. Am I in your way?' I enquired.

'Oh, that's all right,' he answered in a surprisingly strong voice, pointing to his small rowing boat. 'I'm just going to check on my pots. You take the front.'

We worked together to move the boat. I was surprised and delighted – he seemed far too old to be going to sea alone. After this I noticed a number of senior citizens moving around with great purpose. It all seemed a far and happy cry from the herds of old folk drifting around the Channel Islands. Perhaps there is such a relish for life here that age presents no need for compromise.

 I should have let John do the washing, then he might have ended up on the stage of St Mary's town hall, wearing a nightie and singing 'Always Look Under the Bed in Case There's a Man There'. The trouble is I'm too chatty, and so is the splendid Maggie who runs the launderette.

Lots of people come to the Isles because of their beauty. Maggie first arrived thirty-two years ago for a summer holiday under the mistaken impression that she was going to Sicily in Italy. She came for the summer, fell in love and stayed on. Now she lives for the Scillonian Entertainers, an am-dram group of such renown that they entertain tourists all summer long. Before I could so much as apply softener to my whites I was backstage, about to take part in the show. John bought a ticket. Swine.

Row upon row of colourful frocks was being raided as the company prepared. The welcome I received was second to none and put Alderney firmly from my mind. We had a show to do. Rapidly coached in the words of the song, I hurriedly put on a borrowed nightie and headed for the wings. It wasn't until I was on stage that I realized everyone else had bare feet and I still had my boating shoes on. If I say so myself, we were a big hit, but there was no time to rest on our laurels. I had to get ready for the lifeboat sketch. Discussion ensued about my role. Perhaps I might play a drowning victim? Jacky, who'd held the candle in the nightie song, shook her head.

'That might be all right if one of the women had been doing the sketch,' she confided. 'But it's Richard and Philip, you see, they're just not versatile. You'll have to be a lifeboat man.' I donned yellow oilskin and sou'wester.

As the women trooped through another number, I waited backstage with a gentleman in his underpants. Theatrical people are very chatty in their smalls. I can't say I was surprised to find out he was the Chief of Police. I'd just been passing the time with a merchant banker dressed as Wee Willie Winkie. The Chief tucked his bleeper away and put on a sailor-suit. He'd once been doing a show, dressed as a Spaniard, when his bleeper had gone off and he'd dealt with the crime enquiry dressed in bolero and false moustache. It would give a criminal a bit of a start to have Don Quixote turn up and start doing knee-bends with the words 'Hello, hello, what've we got 'ere, then?'

Philip and Richard turned out to be not at all versatile. We carried on our cardboard lifeboat to the tune of 'Who Will Man the Lifeboat?' and they promptly stepped on both my feet simultaneously. I couldn't remember the words and was saved only by the appearance of Britannia dressed in an old sheet and a cardboard helmet, who came on to bring the curtain down. Wild applause was followed by Jacky's demand: 'All right! Who sent the sea on upside down?'

Checking the listings for tonight's rave on the Isles of Scilly.

JOHN The show was great fun, full of enthusiasm and vitality. I was particularly impressed by the performance of a small blonde woman singing the chorus of 'Who Will Man the Lifeboat?'. She seemed vaguely familiar.

DAY 11 Isles of Scilly

JOHN Tom's anxious to change *Hirta*'s oil so we're staying in St Mary's today. The sun is still shining! St Mary's is very peaceful, the public gardens full of palm trees and other exotic vegetation. It's warm and the air is filled with birdsong.

SANDI John and I started the morning with a coffee in the Corner House Restaurant in Hugh Town. It's one of those places where a lot of old ladies take tea and anybody bold enough to have a conversation knows that it must be done in an obligatory whisper. The Scilly Isles may be free and easy but they still

The ancient graveyard of Old Town Church.

47

share the Eleventh Commandment which God gave only to Britain – Thou shalt not be heard talking aloud in a public place. The temptation to behave badly was almost too much. Fortunately, some Americans came in and did it for us. 'Oh, Harry, isn't this adorable!' announced a large lady in check trousers ready to test the elasticity of her waistband. The locals gulped their refreshments and departed.

Out of Hugh Town are the country lanes, hedgerows and the twittering birds which normally only appear in BBC plays. Past Harold Wilson's grey, low bungalow (he may have been a decent Prime Minister but clearly he had no sense of décor) we walked down a dirt path with overhanging trees and dense blackberry bushes. Any minute Ma Larkin would appear with a pitcher of fresh lemonade. A field of potatoes led through to the ancient graveyard of the old parish church. Here the gravestones bore extraordinary stories.

There was Captain Newman of the *Invincible* who died of yellow fever, aged twenty-one, on a passage to the Cape of Good Hope. Must have been a job getting him back. One sailor, a surgeon, had been buried standing up facing the sea and forever looking at Old Town Bay, Tolmen Point, and Gull Rock off Lundy Island.

Matt and Richard Lethbridge, local brothers in their later years, came down to meet us at the church. Richard and I were by way of being old colleagues. He's a portly gentleman with astonishing Denis Healey eyebrows. The night before he'd been strutting his stuff in a bright pink, silk bow tie and cummerbund as Chairman of the Scillonian Entertainers. Matt is the most decorated coxswain of the RNLI. His weather-beaten face was pure relaxation as he pushed his white peaked cap on to the back of his head and jutted his strong arms out from his red tartan, short-sleeved shirt.

He was rather disparaging about the many awards and medals that he's been given. He said the people who give them wouldn't know whether you were brave or not. He concluded: 'The people who know you know it's a lie and the people who don't, well, it doesn't really matter.' His eyes sparkle when he talks about the sea. He says it affects their whole lives. 'It even affects the girls' monthlies,' he said shyly. 'If I'm allowed to say that.' When his granddaughter went to Wales for a trip with her school friends from the islands, they spent their time going up and down the hills. They found they were constantly looking for a glimpse of the sea over the brow of each hill.

The old boys were true cracker-barrel philosophers. After about an hour of chat Matt suddenly realized who John was. He slapped the large stone he was sitting on.

'Ah, but what is fame?' he said. 'This stone. Think how long it's been here and what it's seen. And that bit of gravel down there,' and he pointed to the path, 'that's one of us.' And then he laughed as if he'd perhaps said too much.

Sitting in the shade of palm trees overpowered by the sweet smell of wild flowers in the company of these warm, spirited old men it was hard to imagine it being any other way. A winter storm rampaging around the island, disturbing their tranquillity and calling the men to the lifeboats?

'Can you ever get used to danger?' I asked Matt. There was a long pause; he seemed nonplussed by the very idea of danger. Finally he replied in the only way he could: 'Living here, you have to be dependent on yourself – that's what you get from the sea, independence'.

THE SEA

You can be one of the greatest shipmasters in the world but still not be permitted to pilot an inter-island launch around the Isles of Scilly. It takes ten years of training to get to know all the various rocks and reefs which have interrupted many a sea journey.

DAY 12   Isles of Scilly

Our plan to leave today had to be abandoned. The weather has turned again. It has been raining on and off and there is a threat of fog. These islands are paradise in fine weather but getting away from them in bad conditions is a grim prospect. At times like this our commitment to returning to Falmouth for the Classics becomes a burden.

Despite this underlying tension we had another great day exploring another island, St Agnes, the most south-westerly habitation in the UK. We went over in Fraser Hick's launch, *Black Swan*, to St Agnes. Fraser and his fellow boatmen ferry tourists and supplies to this and the other smaller islands.

They build handsome men in the Scilly Isles. The pilot, Fraser, was a bit of a rugged dash but his mate had stepped straight out of 'Heart-throb UK'. A blond Adonis, swathed in yellow oilskins, he appeared to have sprung to life from the logo of some particularly manly aftershave. I explained to my team of boys that this was what foul-weather gear ought to look like. I was not popular.

The seas had turned choppy as we headed out past the romance of the local

ABOVE: *John poses for an aftershave advert.*

LEFT: *Matt Lethbridge, the RNLI's most decorated coxswain.*

place-names – Rat Island, Barrel of Butter and the Doctor's Keys – round the north of St Mary's and on to St Agnes and the small island of Gugh. The old *Swan* ploughed through the waters and dumped several loads of it on John and myself. We weren't just going to sea, we were becoming part of it. With our hair plastered to our scalps, and our wet-weather gear living up to its name, we approached the low waters of St Agnes's quay. In the last of the spring tides the water drops fairly dramatically and we bobbed in, skimming the very bottom of the harbour.

The first thing you see on St Agnes is the pub, The Turk's Head. We made a beeline for it, eager to dry off and get some sustenance. Within minutes we were enjoying spicy soup and Cornish pasties, and being made very welcome by the landlords John and Pauline. There was none of that frosty scrutiny that you so often get going into a strange pub.

THE ST AGNES LIFEBOAT

The first St Agnes lifeboat had a 1000-foot wooden run down into the sea but they didn't quite get the construction right. Consequently it was a little short and the last foot of the trip into the sea was completed by simply dropping into the water. There was also a bump in the middle, about two-thirds of the way down, where all the men had to get out and push before rushing back on the boat and then falling into the sea. Presumably their motto was: 'We'll be with you – in a minute'.

It's too easy when you travel not to give yourself time to take a place in, but the calm beauty of St Agnes insists on recognition. Around most of the island the sea beats continuously on the horizon. It affects even the most jaded. We walked for about ten minutes up narrow lanes to the local school.

'Anyone is welcome to visit,' stated the sign on the door. I don't remember feeling welcome at my school and I was a pupil. The low brick building in front of the lighthouse was awash with brightly painted dragons and daffodils in the windows – not your run-of-the-mill State primary.

Inside the colourfully decorated communal classroom, the ten children who attend the school were scattered about their tasks. At one end of the room the five-year-olds were busy making aeroplanes out of balsa wood. They were happily drilling and sawing their way through the basics of carpentry with no apparent finger loss. Two kids tapped away on computers while the six- and seven-year-olds made small shell animals to sell at the school fête. A paper Viking boat covered an entire wall and finger-puppets and art projects competed for the remaining space. I wanted to sit down and make something straightaway.

Roger Riley, the headmaster, stressed the lack of crime on the island, stating that any child can go out on a Saturday morning and the parents won't worry if they're not back until teatime. The children don't leave for the mainland until their late teens and further education. Young islanders have been known to be overwhelmed by the confusions of modern life and have had to return.

What does this argue in favour of? An innocent, carefree childhood running free amid natural splendour is the bygone dream of many people, but perhaps it is the dream of adults. I was seduced by it. For that moment I wanted things left just as they are on St Agnes. Indeed, I wanted my kids to run out of their door with safety and know that no one would harm them. I wanted the peace of mind which such security brings to grown-ups. But what happens to the growing child? If the small community atmosphere creates adults totally unprepared to face the rest of the world, then in the long run the children may have been done a disservice. They may end up unsuited to anything apart from island life yet, in the future, the island may not be able to sustain them.

A SCILLY FIRST

The Isles of Scilly were the first in the UK to insist on compulsory education. It was a penny a week for each child to go to school and two pennies for them not to. Which is a pretty nifty system of encouragement.

JOHN Sandi and I went for a walk down the other side of the school hill towards the northern edge of the island. A beautiful little house stood empty.

'Make a lovely holiday place,' said Sandi, looking through the window.

I shared her enthusiasm. 'Absolutely, but I don't know … I don't think it would be right just to come here occasionally.'

It was a community and you had to take part. In the distance we could see the sea bashing against the Bishop Rock lighthouse. Beyond that, nothing until America.

'We've reached the edge of Britain,' Sandi said quietly.

I nodded. 'I wonder if anyone in charge ever looks this far on the map.'

SANDI As we strolled on we passed the sign for Danny Hicks's Model Boat Shop. We entered into a tatterdemalion workshop of tools, scraps of wood and the chewed remains of old pencils where Danny creates perfect replicas of ships of all sizes. Pieces of hardened glue and wood splinters flew from his fingertips as he animatedly leafed through his photo album of past work. In it was a model of the ship Robert Maxwell fell off for his unexpected final dip. Danny pointed out that the only place on board where one could easily fall off was a deck area designed only for the crew while operating machinery – an unlikely spot for a ship-owner to take a breather in the middle of a summer's night. I liked the idea of detective work fermenting in this secluded artists' haven.

JOHN Danny's wife Wendy appeared at the door and invited us in for a cup of tea. Like most people on the island, the Hicks take paying guests. Wendy took a break from preparing their supper to chat with us. In their sitting room, both sides of the house looked out to sea. Originally from Warwickshire, Wendy now cannot stand being inland for more than a few days. She said that looking at the sea allows her to be detached from day-to-day problems and to put life in perspective, giving her a better sense of herself in relation to the world around her.

THE COASTGUARD BUILDINGS

The old St Agnes coastguard building is divided into three terraced houses and represents official planning gone to hell. The tower at one end was supposed to overlook the Western Rocks so that the friendly coastguard could do his job properly, but they were designed back to front. When the local builder saw the plans, he wrote to the Ministry concerned and said the building would not overlook the dangerous Western Rocks, or even face the sea, as intended. Instead it gave a marvellously protective view of the flower fields. The Ministry thought about this and decided that it would cost a great deal of money and cause considerable delay to alter the plans, so it went ahead and built it the wrong way. A fine example of outsiders telling the islanders what to do.

SANDI The Hicks's live in the old coastguard buildings. Up at the top of the tiny 5-feet-square look-out tower, you can still see the sea all around. Admittedly the Western Rocks are obscured by three chimneys but it is a romantic place. You ascend an extremely steep and narrow set of wooden steps, somewhere between a ladder and a flight of stairs, to the glazed eyrie. Here one could write or think or philosophize. I dreamt of a quiet summer, slipping fountain pen across pure white paper like some latter-day Vita Sackville-West, writing and writing with the sea lapping against the edge of flower fields while children laughed below as they rushed home from school. John and I sat silent on a narrow windowseat at the top of the tower. Perhaps some places can be small without ever confining you.

THE ST AGNES LIGHTHOUSE

It's now a private house but it has a noble history. The lighthouse is alleged to have saved the life of Benjamin Franklin, either on his way to America or coming back. He was so impressed that he went home and instituted a series of lighthouses up and down the east coast of the United States.

JOHN At the Turk's Head we joined our new friends for supper. The worsening weather had cancelled the local rowing races. The pub kitchen had been left with enough curry for fifty hungry people. Everyone did the decent thing. We all had curry.

SANDI Danny and Wendy came and waved goodbye on the quay. John and I stood for a very long time at the back of the *Black Swan*, waving until St Agnes disappeared from view.

JOHN Tonight, back in St Mary's, I browsed through *The Scillonian* magazine. In his most recent editorial, Clive Mumford writes: 'Ours is a community that palpably cares, is free from crime's worst excesses, knows not the selfishness, violence and cynicism of the big urban centres. We are blessed with sound, if unspectacular, living standards. In short, the daily round is a most pleasant undertaking and a spirit of decency pervades all'. This portrait of Scilly life, given as it was in a slightly old-fashioned style, echoed my impressions.

> 'For all at last return to the sea – to Oceanus, the ocean river,
> like the ever-flowing stream of time, the beginning and the end.'
>
> RACHEL CARSON

DAY 13 Isles of Scilly to Newlyn

SHIP'S LOG: WINDS NORTH-WESTERLY FORCE 3,
SEA STATE ROUGH.

SANDI Another early start. I think I'll stop mentioning them soon. While we were still in the harbour, we could see fog beginning to creep in. Tom was tense and anxious to get away from the islands. It's tough enough to dodge the rocks and obstacles around the islands without upping the stakes with a fog blanket. In haste we sped out of St Mary's without raising the mainsail and hit the roughest waters yet in an area called the Spanish Ledges. The mainsail has a steadying effect, like a kind of keel in the air. In rough seas without it, *Hirta* was screwed every which way. Her tractor engine threatened cardiac arrest as the motion alternately plunged the propeller deep into the sea and then wrested it right out of the water to whirr aimlessly in the air.

There wasn't a member of the crew who did not wish their mothers had never introduced them to solid foods. Except for me. I felt terrific. Exhilarated by the sheer force and energy of the sea, I clung on to the for'ard hatch cover and watched the spray break. I couldn't believe I didn't feel ill. This thrill, combined with my Stugeron tablets, had the unfortunate effect of making me feel rather smug and it was an exercise of will-power that I didn't go around talking about fried egg sandwiches. I felt I had conquered some weak part of myself and was triumphant.

JOHN I was sure it had been a big mistake coming on this trip. The Spanish Ledges, apparently, were the cause of our troubles. I could not give a damn. But for the energy involved in moving an inch I would have rolled over the side and swum back to St Mary's, or not as the case may be. I was beyond caring. I have never been seasick before and, while I did not vomit, I found I had no energy whatsoever and my head felt as if it was filled with sand. I felt helpless and completely without hope.

How long the seasickness lasted I cannot say but it seemed like an eternity. Eventually the boat's motion eased and we raised the mainsail which further improved stability. The wind picked up and we were able to hoist the jib and staysail and were going along at a good speed, *Hirta* crashing through the swell with her gunwales sometimes dipping in the water. I decided to put on a life-jacket. Although I felt safer with it on, going below, albeit for only a minute or two, brought back the dizziness.

My spirits were restored when the sun came out and Tom decided that conditions were good enough to raise the topsail. Trying to maintain your balance and rig and hoist the sail while *Hirta*, heeled well over, raced on through the waves was invigorating.

SANDI It's not easy being the only woman at sea in a crew of seven. My experience so far has shown me that sailing is, without doubt, both in port and at sea, a laddish activity. If I get sick, I lie down to die but the boys have a different approach. The more the waves beat up, the more laddish they all become. All nice fellows but there is a danger that, when they get highly excited and want to start heaving on all the ropes, they just take over and my weaker physical presence has no place. Two weeks into the trip and they have stopped warning me that they're going to pee over the side. They stand at the shrouds and merrily do their business. There is nowhere for me to avoid it. Consequently, I have begun a private survey which I call the DFS, or Distance From Shrouds, in which I assess how close to the edge of the boat each individual needs to stand. Interestingly, they all have very different techniques. Only one of them washes his hands in the sea afterwards. Tom tends to choose the moment just after his DFS to clap me on the shoulder and ask if I'm all right. I wonder if women are generally more fastidious or whether I spent too long at boarding school.

JOHN I was elated at being able to steer the boat successfully to windward. Tom explained that the idea was to get her headed as close as possible to the direction of the wind without going too far and letting the wind catch the other side of the sails and force us to lose speed and tack; I think. The trouble is that I am certain I follow what he is saying at the time but later, when I try to remember, I cannot picture the conditions clearly enough and it all becomes muddled. At times I am simply doing what I did last time, which might be totally inappropriate to the conditions; I just do not have enough experience yet. I am also quite distracted by Tom's fierceness. He is good at apologizing for our mistakes by saying he should have been more explicit in his instructions but, at the time, his temper disturbs my concentration.

A minor blight on this beautiful sail was that we were going in the wrong direction. Instead of heading for the north Cornwall coast, we were going backwards on ourselves just to the east of Land's End on the south coast. Backwards on our journey. When Tom explained that going north-east straight into the strong winds would have involved an even more uncomfortable ride than we had coming out of the Scillies, I became overwhelmed by a desire to see Newlyn. Any frustration at having to make the detour was completely outweighed by the sheer joy of the sailing. It was glorious tacking back and forth across Mount's Bay. The sun lit up the green fields and woods on top of the cliffs and flashed across the water to the fairy-tale majesty of St Michael's Mount in the distance.

In towards Mousehole on the Cornish coast, we skimmed so close to tiny fishing boats that we could see the mackerel on the ends of their hand-pulled lines. At that moment I could have sailed around the world and never stopped for breath.

We were an unusual sight. Newlyn Harbour is almost entirely full of fishing boats moored in serried ranks away from the quay like a great chorus line of fat ladies. We joined a line tying up alongside eight hulking fishing vessels steaming with the aroma of fish, drying nets and diesel. Tomorrow we head for Padstow. Coming up for two weeks on our journey and, who knows, perhaps we will actually leave Cornwall.

DAY 14 Padstow

I am looking forward to a day when I don't have to wear rubber trousers. We have successfully arrived in Padstow, where I have fallen deeply in love. The harbour is one of those places where you could happily buy a postcard from

the 1950s and still get pretty much the same view. Perhaps the shop names have changed but the houses with pitched or Dutch gable roofs have been here for generations. The ancient stone wall runs down to the water's edge where the inner harbour lock gate opens twice a day to release the sheltered shipping.

 Tree-covered hills rise behind the town and there are acres of sand dunes on the far side of the wide estuary of the Camel river. Although there are many cafés and gift shops, Padstow has not lost its identity as a port. *Hirta* is tied up in the inner harbour beside the *Maria Asumpta*, a magnificent two-masted brigantine. Built in 1858, she is the oldest active square-rigged sailing ship in the world and looks more at home here than do the modern yachts. Her deck is buzzing with preparations for the next voyage. The crew, with their pony-tails, bare feet and tallow-drenched cut-off trousers, add to the impression that we have drifted back a hundred years or more.

SEA MUSCLES

It is estimated that one-seventh of the Navy in Nelson's day wore trusses due to hernias resulting from all the rope pulling and hauling.

I proudly proclaim my undying affection for Rick Stein, chef extraordinaire at The Seafood Restaurant, Padstow. Unsure if I would ever cook again, I went shopping for something which could be pre-prepared for the next day's journey to Skomer Island.

At the quayside, 'live fish shop' fishermen can chug their boats right to the back door and chuck in their catch. A large cold cabinet displayed an array of monkfish, brill, plaice, mackerel, herring, smoked salmon, lobster and crab ready to tempt me. In the live fish-tank the terrifying face of a giant conger eel leapt out at me. I decided I didn't want to buy anything quite so violent. So I settled on mackerel instead.

The kitchen at Rick Stein's is like one of those brilliant Heath Robinson machines which look impossible and function brilliantly. A casserole of chefs were getting on with preparations, and each other, around a large central stainless steel cooking area and an enormous Aga. The chef himself was in residence and I proffered my bag of mackerel.

'I want to be able to eat it cold or be able to reheat it the next day.'

'Ah,' he said, 'you want Mackerel Escabèche.' In an instant orders were given, fish filleted and sensuously salivating smells began rising. As he cooked, Rick bemoaned British cooking. He could not understand how this nation could have so many wonderful ingredients and yet be unable to prepare good food simply. How could Britain, just like Japan, be surrounded by the sea and yet, unlike the Japanese, have such an odd and wary attitude to fish?

For about £2.50, Rick made a healthy and fabulous meal.

MACKEREL ESCABÈCHE

2 mackerel, each weighing 8–10 oz	2 cloves of garlic
6 fl oz olive oil	4 tablespoons wine vinegar
Seasoned flour	4 tablespoons water
2 oz carrot, peeled and thinly sliced	1 teaspoon chopped Greek oregano
2 oz onion, peeled and thinly sliced	Salt and ground black pepper

Fillet the mackerel. Pour half the oil into a large non-stick frying pan. Heat the oil and dust the mackerel fillets with the seasoned flour. Pat off any excess.

Fry the fillets on both sides till golden brown, then transfer them to a shallow dish, which should be just large enough for them to be laid side by side.

Pour the rest of the olive oil into the frying pan and fry the carrot, onion and garlic until they begin to colour. At this point add the wine vinegar, water, oregano and seasoning. Simmer until the vegetables are cooked, then pour the contents of the frying pan over the fish and leave to go cold.

JOHN I was told I shouldn't leave Padstow without visiting the 'Stoneman', Ed Prynn. Turning a corner into the garden of Ed's utilitarian bungalow I was transported back into the mists of time. Here was a collection of standing stones which would shame Stonehenge, even though Ed has only recently put them all in place. He believes each one holds magical powers; from the Angel's runway which towers incongruously over the breeze-block garage to the several tons of his mystical rocking stone, still bearing the scars from the pneumatic drill used to shape it. I could imagine Ed, who is in his late fifties with flowing white hair, as a wizard. He sometimes dresses up in Druid costume to perform rebirthing ceremonies in the underground chamber he built with his partner Glynnis.

Glynnis is not one to be outdone. She has covered the outside walls of the bungalow with engraved stone tablets

A happy woman with seafood chef extraordinaire, Rick Stein.

dedicated to people whom she admires from all times and places. I was very flattered that, amongst Mother Teresa, Margaret Thatcher, Captain Bird's Eye and Buffalo Bill, she had carved one for me. My name hung beside Harry Houdini's. We could have done with him in Beirut.

A small man, Ed moves around with swift jerky movements and, while talking, brings his face very close to stare with great intensity into your eyes. He is blind in one eye and the other is weak following an accident at the quarry where he used to work, but his intensity does not come from myopia: he wants to communicate his sense of wonder at the healing power he feels the stones want him to harness. As he showed me the healing stone circle named after different ladies in his life I was tempted to dismiss him as a phoney or lunatic but my cynicism was defeated by his enthusiasm, humility and warmth of character. He has created a Cornish rival to the Blarney Stone – the Dreckly Stone. Once the stone is touched, he explained, your innermost desires are guaranteed to be realized – 'dreckly'. It seemed far-fetched but I touched the stone several times, just in case.

DAY 15 Padstow to Milford Haven

SHIP'S LOG: WINDS NORTHERLY FORCE 3,
SEA STATE CALM.

 Two weeks now and we haven't reached Wales yet. I've stopped looking at the map. It can't be possible that we plan to travel all that distance. Life has become a preoccupation with keeping dry, awake and alert. As we prepared to set sail at dawn the *Maria Asumpta* was beginning to come to life as well. A fledgling crew had joined her last night, carting sleeping bags and high hopes. Now these innocents were on deck getting their first briefing to begin the mind-boggling process of learning how sailing ships sail. The romance of the high seas is a lot more like hard work than they yet realize.

At 6.30 the lock gates opened. We waited for the green light to clear the harbour and set sail for Skomer Island. Tom was very glad to get out safely. The buoys mark a very narrow channel here and the sands shift constantly below you, so you can never be entirely sure whether you're on the right course or not. It seems to be a very tense business, sailing.

 Sandi and I hoisted the jib and staysail virtually unaided. We are a lot more confident now we've found our sea-legs. However, we are very aware that our sail-hoisting technique lacks elegance. Our triumph was almost destroyed by

59

gales of laughter: at one point, Sandi shrieked 'You're Johnny Jib,' and as I turned aft to acknowledge the acclamation she continued 'and I'm Sandi Staysail!' She was hopeless with mirth, hugging the sail to untie its lashing, looking rather like a koala bear in a eucalyptus tree.

It was cold and cloudy but there was a good breeze coming in from the north-east and we raced along at 6 or 7 knots. Although 7 knots is only a gentle jogging speed on land it seems very fast at sea and there is a profound satisfaction in using the wind's power against the water through the sails and hull. Learning the ancient and elementary art of sailing – of hoisting sails and tying off ropes, grasping the basics of navigation and holding a course – is all very rewarding. Water occasionally sprayed over the deck but I relished sitting up in the bow as we rode the waves, wondering if this was how a jockey felt going over the sticks.

When the sky cleared at midday and the sun beat down, warming the smooth deck timbers, I knew I was hooked. This really was what I had dreamed of for so long: even the awareness of the clock ticking away for Falmouth could not detract from the sheer pleasure of the moment. It seemed appropriate for this feeling to come while crossing the Bristol Channel where *Hirta* had served her years as a working pilot cutter.

SANDI There are few safe havens north of Padstow before you hit Skomer Island off the Pembrokeshire coast. It's an odd thing that here we are cruising around the coast of Britain and yet we have primarily, so far, seen mostly vast expanses of open water and very little coastline. This journey was no exception. The Bristol Channel is the largest estuary in Britain and it certainly feels like it. Water, water everywhere and hardly anything to look at. Once we had left Padstow behind us we were heading out into open water. Morale was good. We had Rick Stein's mackerel to look forward to and it was the most beautiful sunny day.

JOHN Sandi and I made breakfast together. Cooking on board is a contact sport and we're now in the premier league. With our extra layers of clothing we bounce against each other constantly while a wide strap keeps us within the confines of the galley.

'Tomatoes?'

'Lovely. Sorry.'

'No, my fault. Bacon's nearly ready. Sorry.'

'Ow!'

'Sorry.'

'No problem. Oops! Sorry.'

Generally we can now make the boat's motion work for us. There's a trick to it. If you want to collect something from the other side of the saloon, you just wait for the right wave and then launch yourself with its motion. This way, you can arrive in one pace instead of six.

SANDI I've taken to keeping packets of Stugeron concealed about the boat and have become a bit of a secret pill-popper. I want to test myself on this journey but not enough to give up the tablets. I've never been into drugs. I was always afraid if I tried something I might actually like it. I wonder if there are meetings for Stugeron addicts?

When you are at sea and water is constantly all around you it is very easy to become deadened by it. The horizon, so beloved of Wendy Hicks on St Agnes, is almost too grand and quite often I find the slate-grey colour acts as a depressant. You look around you and there's just water as far as you can see with no real form and no hint of land to warm you or relieve the eye. It's not like travelling through countryside where different aspects will catch your attention. The sea's the sea and once you've settled down to it being a force 4 or whatever, there really isn't very much to look at. Most of us find that reading is impossible and snakes and ladders is absurd. We all talk a great deal but mostly in shifting pairs which always leaves some solitary time. My restless nature finds the confines hard. I have never done well exploring the quieter caverns of my mind. I am constantly conscious of John's captivity and aware that any complaints about life on board are mere whingeing compared with his ordeal. We are all easier with each other now and it is better. When we meet people they tend to treat John like a card-house which might collapse at any moment. It's good to see the crew beginning to tease him like they would anyone else. We are starting to settle into comfortable friendships which helps the long, wet days. We all sleep more than usual.

JOHN I was steering towards Skomer mid-afternoon. 'Look at my monkey's fist!' said Sandi, who is rapidly becoming a rope bore. Just then I saw a flash of grey and white well ahead, off the starboard bow. Soon we had a school of porpoises playing around the bows, so close you could hear them breathing when they broke the surface. They stayed a minute or two, then vanished as quickly as they had come. Just after these sea-hogs, as sailors of old christened them, had gone, a pigeon landed on the deck. Tom hates this, having seen previous sick refugees die slowly after making a mess of his deck; but this one flew away safely when we got closer to the land. We had seen nothing all day, save one ship far away on the horizon, yet within moments we were visited by creatures from above and below.

SANDI Pol showed me the trick of pulling up on the purchase halyards. Now this is not something I ever thought I'd get excited about but I have been very aware of being the weak female on board and am delighted to learn anything which helps me pull my weight. This is literally about pulling my weight. The purchase halyards act as the final tightening for a raised sail and much of the work is really just a technique. You hook the rope underneath a belaying pin. One person holds the end of the rope while you grab the middle. You then drop your weight back, pull the rope to you and, as you push it forward, your chum takes up the slack. I love it. I happily bounce right down to the deck and watch contentedly as yards of slack pull through.

Each day there is a new job which we're accomplishing and we grow in pride and pleasure at becoming useful on board. No one wants to be a passenger – it's too boring just coming along for the ride.

DISCONCERTING FOLKLORE OF THE SEA
'When the sea-hog jumps, stand by the pumps.'

JOHN Late afternoon the sky clouded over behind us, suggesting no way back, and ahead there were shifting shades of white, grey and black, threatening danger. After twelve hours at sea we could see our destination, the island of Skomer. However, the elements had other ideas. The wind had moved round to the north and was blowing dead on our nose, making the anchorage off Skomer too exposed. Tom decided that we should head for shelter behind St Ann's Head near Milford Haven. It means we will lose more time. It is frustrating having to change the plans so often.

SANDI Amidst grumbling, we changed course to our new destination. It would take at least two hours so I decided to make supper. This was a mistake. Tom thundered that he hadn't given the order for food. It was news to us that when and what we ate had to be authorized. On deck, the wind had picked up a bit and I took the wheel as we rounded the lighthouse at the haven entrance. We were sailing to windward and I tried to relax into the challenge of keeping *Hirta* at maximum pace. It is a wonderful feeling not to be sailing by compass-bearings but to take her along into the wind and then out again. Your whole being can feel when she's happy as you check the sails and judge the moody wind. In the distance we could see the oil industry which the name of
Milford Haven brings to mind, but here was   OPPOSITE: *Learning the ropes.*

62

undeveloped peace. In the perfect light of a summer's evening, we skimmed under sail to an anchorage across calm waters. The noise of an engine would have been an insult.

As we tidied the sails away my hands felt weary and ached. Tom put up an ancient anchor lamp at the bow. We were the only stroke of colour on a dark canvas. At a quarter past ten we finally had supper. The diversion had taken over three hours and everyone was completely exhausted. We lit the paraffin lamps in the saloon and opened the excellent Sauvignon from Rick Stein's. Everybody became much jollier as Tom got his guitar and started singing. We have too far to journey to end in temper now.

Supper in the saloon.

The diversion was worth it; the setting sun lit up the sea and the high cliffs around the vast expanse of Milford Haven beautifully. After a good meal, plenty to drink and Tom's singing it became very cheerful in the saloon with the fire belting out heat and the oil lamps bringing a warm glow to the polished wood. It was not cosy on deck. Some time after midnight I went up for a last cigarette before turning in. It was freezing.

Milford Haven, Skomer and Solva

SHIP'S LOG: WINDS NORTH/NORTH WESTERLY FORCE 4 OR 5,
SEA STATE CALM.

JOHN I felt lousy this morning: bleary with a hangover and incredulous that we were up at six again and underway for Skomer and its bird sanctuary within the hour. I wanted only to sleep and cursed tides and winds for always commanding departures at dawn.

SANDI The omnipotent radio shipping forecast woke us at ten to six. I could hear John groaning below me, while the chaps in the saloon slowly creaked back into life. As the morning activity reluctantly wound up John and I lay in our bunks whispering like naughty children knowing we should be about our business. There is no place for private conversation in our new home. By the time we appeared on deck the sun had come up. Even with sleep in my eyes it did look absolutely magnificent.

I wish there were a shower. The for'ard loo sits amidst the tar brushes and hemp coils of the rope locker. It's difficult to do anything in there. A swipe round with a wet wipe and a change of pants is not quite my idea of morning ablutions but as I took my toothbrush up on deck the beauty of the morning made it a privilege to be there.

JOHN Fortunately the cool breeze soon cleared my head and the brilliant flashes of sunlight across the water revived my spirits. We approached Skomer cautiously through Jack Sound as the tide raced against us. The changes on the water's surface in this narrow channel with rocks on either side were spectacular: areas of water rippling and bubbling around pools of slack water that looked like ice. I was fascinated but became aware of the real dangers when *Hirta*'s engine missed a beat. Without that power we would be wrecked. The engine quickly picked up again. My heart took a little longer.

Skomer is an extraordinary sight, with sheer cliffs rising to a plateau at around 200 feet. The skies were teeming with bird life; gulls, fulmars and guillemots swooped and screeched above us. Comical puffins eyed us quizzically as we anchored in the North Haven (a beautiful bay), blew up the rubber dinghy and went ashore. The warden, Steve Sutcliffe, waited on shore with his wife, Anna, and their small son, Benjamin.

Walking around the island you see clear outlines of ancient fields. These and the

remains of buildings date back more than 4000 years and, as they have not been ploughed over by later generations, offer a fascinating and rare insight into the lifestyle of our ancestors.

The island is run by the Dyfed Wildlife Trust, whose appeals for more funds from the Welsh Office will fall on deaf ears unless it can be shown that the island is making a profit. Skomer cannot do this; it has to limit visitors and any new buildings to protect the birds. When a member of the House of Lords visited the island and was told that there were more than 150 000 shearwaters alone during the breeding season, he thought the number excessive and suggested that it would be sensible, good sport and profitable to boot, to have a shooting season.

SANDI As we reached the crest of a small hill, we could see bluebells running wild with their red campion chums. They twine in every hue of purple flung across the grassy, green and brown slopes and warming the grey slate rocks. The island is not quite the echoing emptiness we were expecting. An assistant warden is in full-time residence and so too is a shifting population of scientists. Guillemot and kittiwake counts and breeding research are forever being meticulously carried out by those who find these things endlessly gripping. There's one man, Tim, who has spent twenty-five years studying the Skomer vole, a tiny little russet rodent unique to the island. Twenty-five years. It's not that big an island. I believe he knows every vole personally. I shouldn't be at all surprised if he's been invited to certain vole family occasions.

JOHN I had never been much interested in birds before meeting Steve and Anna but, inspired by their enthusiasm, I found myself eagerly trying to identify the different species.

SANDI *My Twitching Section*

The Black-backed Gull

A bastard in the bird world. There are no ground predators on the island but the black-backed gull makes up for it. It's a huge thing. A real Christmas dinner of a bird and it will eat absolutely anything. As we walked, we heard a childlike cry of pain and looked across a field to see a gull plunging its claws into a rabbit. Steve was adamant that they never interfere with the cruel realities of nature. I'm sure he's right but my pathetic core wanted to run across the field shouting 'Let go of Flopsy, you swine!'

OPPOSITE: *Skomer Island.*

67

The Guillemot

Now, he's cute. A vet friend of mine once bemoaned human beings' reactions to wild creatures. 'It's the survival of the cutest, not the fittest, which reigns these days,' he said. The tiny guillemot looks like a mini-penguin. I guess there are spiders and snakes which merit more attention in the natural chain of things but my heart couldn't help but slip a donation to the guillemot.

The baby guillemots are extremely fluffy and when they're ready to fly the father goes down to the lower part of the cliff-face while the mother stands next to her chicks. Both parents then encourage the young to jump off. It must be quite a daunting sight to stand on a cliff with the sea below you and your Dad screaming: 'Go on, son, you know you can do it.'

Puffins

Avoiding vast patches of thistles, we sat on the edge of the cliff for a while. A noise seemed to be coming from under John's bottom. Anna said he'd sat on the home of another bird, a shearwater. A puffin eyed us over his colourful beak. I was sitting on his burrow. Busy neighbourhood. Puffins are good at flying and rubbish at landing. Their bright orange flippered feet flail out behind them as they dive in for a crash landing. Their brilliant tangerine beaks have little yellow hinges at the sides. It's a good life on Skomer. One of them actually yawned in front of us and showed he was bright orange on the inside of his mouth as well. Clearly their design originally came from some avant-garde art college.

Shearwaters

Skomer has the third largest population of shearwaters in Britain. There are thousands of pairs living on the island so it must be pretty damn crowded wherever the largest population hangs out. Steve showed us an incubating egg. The babies eventually fly to Argentina on their own. This seems incredible. How do they know which way to go? I can get lost 100 yards from home.

On a steep-shored cliff-face kittiwakes, gulls and guillemots had created a condominium of bird heaven. The combined bird noise was like sitting inside the speakers at a Jean-Michel Jarre concert but come August they all depart for South America and places adjacent for the winter, and the island becomes silent. The birds only visit land to breed. They're sea birds. They prefer to sit on the sea and rest but childbirth would be tricky like that. In the distance we could see the island of Grassholm, half of which appeared to be covered in white chalk. It is in fact the largest gannet population in the world living very very close to each other. Must have a job cleaning up when there's company.

The Sutcliffes will soon be leaving Skomer – with regret and only for economic reasons. Steve's salary is absurdly small and he couldn't afford to turn down a better offer on the mainland. It seems ridiculous that a place of such natural and historic importance should rely on selfless enthusiasts to have any chance of survival.

 We were late and the tide now hated us. It's not just *Hirta*'s length which dictates where she can go. There's also a surprisingly large amount of boat under the water (an 8 inch draft if we're being technical), so we needed to stooge around until the next high tide helped us up around the Lleyn Peninsula. I suggested going across St Brides Bay to the small Pembrokeshire fishing village of Solva, where I've spent many a happy hour. Oddly, everyone thought this was a good idea and we set off. Hard to believe we are able to go somewhere we want to rather than somewhere we're forced to go. The Pembrokeshire coast is one of my favourite parts of the world. I've spent many happy holidays here but never before seen it from the sea. Familiar places made unfamiliar. We sailed close, admiring the strata in the headlands.

'Can you smell that?' asked John, touching my arm.

'Smells like grass,' I said uncertainly.

It was. The smell of fresh green grass drifting across the water. We could imagine Welsh sailors reaching the coast from dangerous voyages and filling their lungs with the first whiff of home. I remembered an episode from John's book. After years in captivity he and Brian Keenan were unexpectedly given a bowl of cherries. They had had nothing like it for a very long time yet they did not devour the cherries instantly; they sat and stared at the fruit because they had not seen the colour red for so long. They needed the colour more than they needed the food.

Solva is a pretty village, rising up from a Norwegian-like fjord. We anchored outside the harbour entrance and took the inflatable in to meet some old friends of mine, Sue and Allen King. It was so wonderfully ordinary to sit in someone's home and chat. Solva is perhaps not the sort of place tourists might immediately be drawn to. It has no particular outward attractions but, once there, its quiet and friendly atmosphere hooks you.

After a shower at Allen and Sue's I felt better prepared for our overnight passage north across Cardigan Bay. By six o'clock this evening we were going through Ramsey Sound, another tidal maelstrom, with Tom guiding *Hirta* gently through the mix of boiling eddies and slow-turning whirlpools. I was transfixed by the changes in the water, aware of how even *Hirta*'s solid construction

would leave us helpless if we lost power. I was amazed to see canoeists racing with the tide among the rocks by the shore. The sun sank slowly behind Ramsey Island, lighting the sky a brilliant pink above low clouds and the dark blue-grey sheen of the water; foreboding yet quite beautiful.

SANDI There is a quiet, companionable air on board but I am gripped by homesickness. The sun glowing on the cinnamon sails, the fresh breeze and the smell of the grass is almost too good. Travelling is best as a shared experience. It is both exciting and wearying. Confucius or somebody said, 'It is better to travel than to arrive,' but I don't think he meant you should travel all the time. It is good to have John to talk to and share things with but it cannot be the same as those nearest to you.

We were to cross Cardigan Bay in the night. Once again it had turned cold and many layers were needed. No watches had been called so I appeared on deck at about 10 o'clock, fully dressed, only to be informed I'd been off-watch since 9.30. Information is at a premium on this vessel.

I tried to get a bit of sleep before being back on duty at half-midnight. There really isn't room for all of us to sleep well on board. I'm in the pipe cot above John's

ABOVE: *Shrouds.*

OPPOSITE: *A bowsprit moment.*

bunk because it's the only berth left and I'm the only one who fits. It's a curious affair, a piece of cloth, just the width of my body, lashed to two pipes and suspended from the ceiling with what I hope are well-tied knots. My nose is almost directly under the white-painted wooden ceiling and all night the wooden blocks on the deck clog-dance in the wind. There is no room to turn over and change position; you pick one and stick to it. The last time I slept like this was when I was eighteen and passed through the whole of Yugoslavia sleeping in a luggage rack above the heads of my Inter-Rail companions, a Greek family and several disturbed chickens.

Note to myself: It's a mistake to drink too much before attempting to tie the knots which hold your bed in the air.

 I stood the first three-hour watch with Tom from 9.30. It was bitterly cold but clear enough to see lights along the shore, which was reassuring. Before the light went, a flock of seagulls flew low across our path, going out to sea. Until this morning I had not realized that many birds live permanently out at sea: a strange and bleak existence. I was glad to be swathed in layers of high-tech clothing. Having learnt from experience on the passage to Falmouth, I had everything I needed – gloves, cigarettes and woolly hat – ready to hand and was heartened by the awareness of losing some of my novice's anxieties. When Tom went below to check the charts, I realized I was confident that I could hold our course and keep a proper look-out. I stood on tiptoe to check the compass. I wished I was taller.

DAY 17 — Crossing Cardigan Bay

SHIP'S LOG: LIGHT WINDS, SEA STATE CALM.
0030 HOURS: CHANGE OF WATCH.

Days shouldn't start half an hour after midnight. John woke me from a bubble bath dream. He was tired and cold. In the dark confines of our cabin I dressed as he undressed in mutual silence.

We performed an exotic, rolling *pas de deux* as Sandi struggled into her oilskins and I out of mine; hardly speaking as we lurched about, too tired for pleasantries. I could not be bothered to clear my bunk of a clutter of duffle-bags and camera gear and clambered up into Sandi's tiny pipe cot. It may have looked cosy but was uncomfortable and claustrophobic – my head was inches below the cabin roof. I dozed off only to wake and find myself unbearably hot. I had taken

Pol's advice and left most of my clothes on – in case I was needed urgently on deck – but now shed another layer and slept again.

NIGHT WATCH

Falling asleep on watch would be easy but the punishments used to be severe. In the last century a sleeping sailor could 'be hanged on the bowsprit end of a ship in a basket, with a can of beer, a loaf of bread and a sharp knife, and choose to hang there till he starve, or cut himself into the sea.' Nice.

Pol and I arrived on deck, he as full of schoolboy cheer as ever and me befuddled and no doubt little use. The mainsail was up but the engine throbbed to keep us on course. I took the helm. I couldn't have been more chilled if I had been thrust whole into the vegetable drawer of a particularly efficient fridge. The compass glowed red but below all was dark. The stars beamed bright as we watched the moon rising. It flirted with us, first appearing behind cloud, pink and shy, and then gaining confidence to rise steadily and light the entire bay.

My eyes took time to adjust as they strained at the compass. After a while it got easier. I became aware of the water lapping all around and the emptiness of these seas. We saw nothing at all. No fishing boats, merchant fleets or other mad adventurous people like us. For three hours we drifted alone, eating flapjacks while Pol talked about his childhood. His family had owned *Hirta* before the Cunliffes bought her. He told me about growing up on the boat. Apparently when he and his brothers and sisters were babies, their parents used to shut them in the large drawer in the front cabin in order to stop them rolling around. I think it's good that people are keen on sailing, but there are limits.

Pol's a tall, thin sherbet of a man with prematurely grey hair. Despite being Scottish, he has the kind of English accent which Jeeves would have admired. He also has the longest, most punished feet I've seen outside the Ballet Rambert. In the freezing cold he was barefoot. His family owned Teachers whisky. I'd never met anyone who owned something quite so substantial. My father liked a whisky but he didn't actually own the company.

About half past two we caught the first glimmer from Bardsey Island lighthouse flashing across the waters. Three-quarters of an hour later we saw the shadow of land. I willed us towards it. Watch change. Below, the boys were fast asleep and I groped my way to bed in the dark. My brain and body had ceased communicating, especially with each other. I pulled myself up on to the end of the pipe cot but, as

I tried to lie down, I jammed my head against a beam and wedged my body into an unmovable position. Four in the morning and I'm in the lotus position in rubber trousers. I was convinced that one sudden movement and the others would find me stone dead in the morning with a broken neck. When I was finally free I fell into an instant and dreamless sleep.

 Three-thirty came too quickly and, though fortified by a cup of coffee from Sandi, I stumbled furiously through the saloon cursing the film-crew as they slept soundly through the cold night. The sunrise dissipated my rage: coming up over the northern tip of Cardigan Bay it appeared first as an orange fireball, then turned into a colossal hot-air balloon.

 You have to cross Caernarfon Bar at just the right moment or you'll get stuck. We were early. It's fatal to be early. Almost as bad as being late. We would have to wait.

We found ourselves alongside a neat little bay called Porth Dinllaen Lleyn and dropped anchor. On either side of the bay we could see two small groups of

buildings. My binoculars diligently searched for the word 'pub' without success. It was only ten o'clock in the morning but John and I couldn't face hours of sitting on board going stir-crazy. We set off in the inflatable and landed on the beach.

 Sandi and I pulled the dinghy up on to the sand and looked around. The place was packed with holiday-makers.

'John,' whispered Sandi. 'Everyone's staring at us. Maybe they recognize you.'

'I don't think so.' I pointed to her layers of foul-weather clothing. 'I think they think we're mad.'

OPPOSITE: *Dawn over Bardsey Island lighthouse.*

RIGHT: *John arriving incognito at Porth Dinllaen.*

Everyone was in swimming costumes – except us, still dressed for the chill breeze outside the bay; we must have looked very suspicious.

It was a typical British seaside scene with parents sunbathing and keeping a watchful eye on children playing cricket and building sand-castles. In the absence of any amusement arcades or fun fairs it was very peaceful.

SANDI A red house proclaimed itself a pub called the Tychoch Inn. It's Welsh for the Red House, which is convenient. I tried the door.

'What are you doing?' demanded a small woman behind me.

I jumped. 'Sorry. Do you know when the pub opens?'

'I'm the landlady, Bryony.'

We had struck gold. I asked her if she might make up a lunch to take away. She said she hadn't got any paper plates so she gave us seven china ones. Unexpected kindness is always surprising.

JOHN The pleasure of our unexpected feast was shattered when Tom became incensed at some plastic mugs that Sandi had bought. He thought he would look ridiculous if he was seen letting us use the things, especially as they had 'Captain' and 'Cabin Boy' stencilled on them. It should not have been important but Tom's reaction was so furious that we were all upset.

SANDI *Hirta* is old and so too are the chipped and ragged mugs we've been drinking out of night and day. When your place of work and your home become one there are some small comforts which grow to be important. The non-sailing fraternity decided we'd rather have some new, clean mugs. I pulled out some I'd bought as a joke ages ago. It is hard to describe the furore this caused. Like naughty schoolchildren, we were banned from our mugs. John says he spent five years being forced to drink from a plastic mug and it's hard to imagine how someone would want to stop him from choosing to do so now.

SAILING TIP
Avoid taking initiative.

JOHN Such minor concerns keep flaring up out of all proportion and though things are made up later they are a real drain on everyone's energies. I can imagine that Tom's responsibilities for the boat and for keeping us on schedule weigh very heavily, but such outbursts of temper only serve to undermine us. It is a bit of a nightmare veering from times of genuine strong team-spirit to periods of tense diffidence or downright confrontation. I keep feeling I should do something about this, having had so much experience at dealing with people at close quarters in difficult circumstances, but I just don't have the energy and have decided to concentrate on the job of sailing instead.

Fortified by Bryony's lunch we set sail again. Caernarfon Bar is a movable feast, its sandbanks shifting with every storm, so the chart served little purpose and we had to follow the channel markers carefully.

'Buoy six – green on your starboard bow,' called Sandi from the bow where she lay crouched with her binoculars.

'Six – starboard,' I confirmed, enjoying the concentration needed to steer an exact course – keeping the red buoys to port and the green ones to starboard while heeding Tom and Sandi's warnings about on-coming traffic.

We had hoped to get through the Menai Strait and reach Conwy in one go but the tide would make that route hazardous so we stopped for the night at Port

Dinorwic above Caernarfon. We had successfully negotiated another navigational hazard, and another day.

 # Port Dinorwic to Conwy

SHIP'S LOG: WINDS LIGHT, VARIABLE.

JOHN On through the Menai Strait, the narrow waterway between Anglesey and mainland Wales. Quite an experience. Tom took the helm to negotiate what are alleged to be some of the most dangerous waters in the whole of the British Isles, an area alarmingly called the Swellies. It involved taking *Hirta* frighteningly close to the shore at one point and then shooting under the Menai Bridge. Once through the Swellies we could relax and enjoy looking at Bangor pier and the mountains of Snowdonia rising far into the distant haze. We were surrounded by other yachts sailing or lying at their moorings. I quizzed Tom and Pol, who is a yacht broker, constantly about the boats that took my fancy; I must have set my heart on fifty so far. My excitement at the prospect of owning one was only slightly diminished when I reflected on how much I still have to learn.

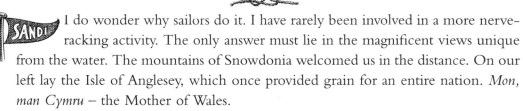

SANDI I do wonder why sailors do it. I have rarely been involved in a more nerve-racking activity. The only answer must lie in the magnificent views unique from the water. The mountains of Snowdonia welcomed us in the distance. On our left lay the Isle of Anglesey, which once provided grain for an entire nation. *Mon, man Cymru* – the Mother of Wales.

Everything was calm until we reached Conwy Marina, when suddenly all hell broke loose. I was asked to pull on a rope at the front. As usual the order was indistinct and I didn't know which rope and didn't like to ask. When I finally discovered the thing, it was caught under the staysail. I threw a rope to Pol, it dropped in the water. He had to stick his foot in the water to try to grab it, and general mayhem and shouting ensued.

JOHN We both felt humiliated as we struggled to get the right mooring ropes to the right places while Tom shouted commands at us. Sandi and I have discussed what happened and have determined to ask for more detailed briefings of our roles before any manoeuvre is started.

We have time to kill waiting for the next tide so we visited Conwy Castle, a magnificent thirteenth-century edifice sitting high above the town. Sandi has an

insatiable appetite for obscure facts and figures. As we walked around the castle to the haunting strains of a busking pipe player, Sandi regaled me with an encyclopaedic variety of details concerning the castle.

 SANDI The guide books will tell you that it's one of Europe's finest surviving examples of a medieval walled borough. The castle is a very solid bit of stuff on a very solid bit of land. It was built in 1283 by Edward I as part of his plan to subdue the Welsh princes. He managed the whole pile with eight large towers for a mere fifteen thousand pounds. Less than the cost of my first flat. Of course, it's

CERDYNPOST RHIF 4.
Dyma ddarlun cerdynpost o gonwy.

the equivalent of nine million pounds today. It's now grey but when it was first knocked up they whitewashed it. Must have looked magnificent: this dominating white castle set against the green fields of Wales and the blue waters of the River Conwy below. A powerful symbol of the domination by the English princes. All around us we could hear snatches of Welsh being spoken. I suspect the princes would have a tougher time of it today. It was so good to be out and stretching our legs.

JOHN We inspected Britain's smallest house in detail; it took nearly a minute.

SANDI The house is a one-up one-down, not just because it only has two rooms but because, if a couple lived there, one of you would have to be upstairs to make any room downstairs. There used to be a 6-foot 3-inch man living here. Probably didn't throw a lot of parties.

Outside, a table displayed the worst collection of tacky souvenirs I've ever seen.
'Isn't it ghastly?' asked John, turning away.
'Yep,' I said, and got my money out.

It seems that Britain is a nation of holiday-makers who wish to recall their break from routine with a pair of nail-clippers and a fridge magnet shaped like a leek.

Conwy to Liverpool

SHIP'S LOG: LIGHT WINDS,
SEA STATE SLIGHT.

SANDI I'm sitting on the bowsprit as we put Conwy behind us and head across Liverpool Bay to its namesake city. The Welsh mountains are just slightly shrouded in mist behind us as we head off in search of the River Mersey. Once again, a vast expanse of sea with not a single ship in sight. I thought Liverpool was one of the great shipping centres of Britain? How can there be no boats in the bay? There might as well have been a silent Armageddon for all the contact we have with the outside world.

JOHN Following our poor display at the marina we got Tom to take us through the complexities of hoisting the topsail before we did it. His explanation was thorough and I now have some understanding of how it works.

SANDI The topsail's a complicated business. I have no idea how it works. There's the downhaul, the leader, the leader which becomes the downhaul, the clew. More jargon, more learning. I wonder if the EEC will make sail boats standardize their names so I shall have learnt all this for nothing.

I'm beginning to feel more comfortable walking about on the boat. Less like standing on my Dad's feet for the rumba. I've got two jackets on, a sweater, thermals, sweatpants and the endlessly sexy waterproof trousers. I haven't bothered with the life-jacket. I reckon no inflatable in the world could keep me and that little wardrobe afloat.

My breakfasts are getting more advanced but it takes about an hour and a half to fry enough for seven hungry people in one pan. There are a lot of other things you can do in an hour and a half. It's quite tricky keeping the frying pan level on the cooker. It's not gimballed, which is not a quality I've ever looked for before in kitchen equipment. Consequently, on a port tack, all the fat just sits jeering at your

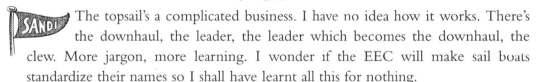

79

food on one side of the frying pan until you come round and the spitting oil shoots over to the other side.

We're just beginning to see some buildings through the lifting rain. I am damp in my dry places and drenched in my damp places. It's one way to keep clean. It has been an incredibly long day with little to do. Tom had been asleep for most of the morning on the starboard saloon bunk.

'Fancy a bowsprit moment?' said John.

We've found that the bowsprit at the front of the boat provides the only place for a quiet chat. Being nautical had gone to my head.

'Shall we have a tot of rum?' I suggested. We sat snugly at the bow, sipping and giggling together.

'So what's Brian Keenan like?' I asked John, looking forward to our planned trip to Ireland to see him.

'He won't approve of your drinking. Never touches a drop.'

We toasted the dear boy as Tom appeared on deck, scowling at our behaviour.

John nudged me. 'After you on the gangplank.'

HISTORICAL NOTE

After the Second World War, the government is alleged to have encouraged women's magazines to produce recipes which took a long time to prepare. This meant women had less time for anything else and spent more time back in the home where they belonged. Would have been easier to make them all cook at sea.

JOHN By the time we had crossed Liverpool Bay the sun had gone, there was mist and drizzling rain – a typical British summer. A red, unmanned lightship marking the 12-mile passage into the docks confirmed we were on course, giving us a dreary welcome with its electronic foghorn. Visibility was down from the usual 20 or so miles to 2 and making out the buoys ahead of us was tricky. With a boat of *Hirta*'s size we had to head for the working docks and radio for a pilot to guide us in.

SANDI As the pilot boat appeared in the mist I was told to steer an extremely steady course and under no circumstances to even glance at the pilot boat. Her crew are very experienced at boat-to-boat transfers and it was up to them to make the connections. My eyes fixed on the buoy ahead as if hypnotized. Which is why I didn't actually see the boat hit us. I think Tom and I both used the same expletives

Sandi's clear view ahead from the helm.

simultaneously. Although minor, the damage was sufficient to draw everyone on board to the starboard side where I was supposed to be keeping an eye on my steady course. The crush of people included Tom, who was now blocking my view with his rather large frame. I was delighted to hand over to the pilot, Alec.

 Solidly built, with a shock of grey hair and rather cold, fishy eyes, Alec is a bluff man. I found it hard to warm to him, sensing that he somehow disapproved of us. He was, however, happy to talk about his work and was proudly defensive of Liverpool. He emphasized that, since container-ization, more goods are being moved through the docks than ever before, despite a drop in the workforce from over 15 000 to just 800 people.

Alec was at the helm as we sailed through the entrance to Gladstone Dock and gave Tom another shock when he clipped the tip of *Hirta*'s bowsprit against the lock wall. It hadn't been a good day for steering.

DAY 20 Liverpool

Liverpool docks are a curious mix: some bustling with activity, others long-idle with weeds growing out of decaying warehouse roofs and rubbish blowing freely in the street. Stacks of imported coal and scrap metal dominated. Alec had emphasized that the port has a bigger throughput than ever but it seemed to lack soul. The anonymous containers concealing who knows what cargo are moved by large robotic cranes across people-less wharves.

The city itself is welcoming, if strange. You can be walking down a street full of smart shops or grand buildings housing shipping companies and Admiralty offices, then turn a corner and find yourself in a run-down backstreet which looks like a mugger's paradise. The people were friendly and cheerful but I couldn't get used to the sudden shifts in the city's appearance.

We have received a severe blow from the weather. The wind has become gale-force, whipping up mountainous seas. We will be going nowhere for a day at least. Our meeting with Brian Keenan across the Irish Sea is looking impossible.

Once notorious on the variety circuit, the Liverpool Empire is still a helluva theatre to play. If a Liverpudlian audience don't think you're up to it they give you 'the bird' and you don't last another minute. Beryl Reid got the bird here when she was sixteen and spent a career making sure it never happened again. It's one of the few places I've improvised where the great fear is that the audience will be funnier than you are. I'd risk it again though, just to step out on to the stage. The Empire has 2300 seats, each one looking close and intimate, but climb up to the back of the circle to look down and you realize what a trick of the eye that is from the stage. The place is huge.

I was nervous taking John there. It meant so much to me that he should like it and that he should feel the same goose bumps that just the dusty smell backstage always gives me.

Walking backstage at the Liverpool Empire was like walking on to the deck of a huge land-bound sailing ship. We climbed up on to the fly-floor, high above the stage, where the fly men bring in the scenery. After three weeks at sea, I felt at home. The same sort of ropes, the same knots, cleats for belaying and the same names. I watched the stage crew going about their chores. With their long hair pulled back in rubber bands, scruffy clothes and a slightly unwashed look, they might all have come off the *Maria Asumpta*.

Most of the first theatres were built in the busiest towns and, in Britain, that meant sea ports. The backstage was staffed by casual labour which, in a port, generally meant out-of-work sailors. They approached the job as if they were at sea: using bowlines, half-hitches, working with hemp and receiving their orders by whistle from below. The signals were the same whether they came from a bos'n or a stage manager. From that day to this it has been bad luck to whistle on the stage. Not a silly superstition. It might bring a piece of scenery down on your head.

Sandi took me out on stage, where she has performed, to get a feel of the whole theatre. The auditorium is vast. I shuddered at the thought of appearing before such an enormous audience. I tried to imagine improvising.

'What on earth do you say when you first come out?' I asked her.

'"Good Evening" is a good start.'

'Of course.'

I tried it but I don't think they'd have heard me in the first row. Stage fright would seem inappropriate here; utter terror would be more the thing. I don't know how she does it.

LIVERPOOL

POSTCARD NUMBER 5:
*Liverpool's modern image of
its bustling self. (Note the
age of the cars.)*

DAY 21 Liverpool

SHIP'S LOG: GALE-FORCE WINDS,
SEA STATE VERY ROUGH.

The place to get proper grub in Liverpool is Stan Hughes's café down on the Dock Road. From the outside you might not think it's quite the thing: a small wooden building held together by peeling paint. In America it would be the heritage site of a revered diner. In Britain it is a celebration of the one meal done properly: all-day breakfast.

Inside, three women – one tiny, one medium-sized and one large – preside like the three little bears of catering. Dressed in immaculate blue-chequered uniforms they slice and serve shift after shift of fabulous fry-up. Your table companions depend upon the time of day. From 7 to 8 a.m., it's the coppers off night-shift; 8 to 9 is the bin men, followed swiftly by an hour of postmen. At 10.30 it's time for take-aways, then lunch, and then home at 3 to be back at 5 each morning.

John was already eating when I joined him.

'I got a berth on a cargo ship to Ireland,' he told me.

'Just the one?'

'I'm afraid so.' He was apologetic. 'It's the only way we can include Ireland in the trip. There's a force 8 out there. *Hirta* would never make it. I'm sorry.'

I was disappointed. I had been dreaming of Ireland, of sipping Guinness with Brian Keenan, but it wasn't to be. John patted my arm. 'Have the Ulster fry. That's sort of Irish.'

Inside the café we could hear a gale blowing up from the west. We have already lost two days since Conwy, and our distant deadline now starts to feel more pressing. I will stay with *Hirta*, waiting for conditions to improve.

JOHN We are both despondent at not sharing this stage of the voyage. Sandi looked anxiously out at the rough seas as I waited to leave Gladstone Lock in the container ship *Kirsten*. She knelt on the lock wall and handed down a bottle of Scotch.

'For the skipper, and have some yourself; I think you'll need it.' I was touched by her concern. As I stood on the bridge waving farewell, wild-eyed with fear and too many seasickness pills, I wondered if I really wanted to see Brian this much.

SANDI The *Kirsten* has a German skipper and a Filipino crew. I wonder if they have the same trouble understanding orders that we do. I don't want to be sailing on without John. He is my good companion.

'The birds on the Liver Building, that are unfairly supposed by Liverpool seafarers to flap their wings when passed by a woman of untarnished virtue, wept ceaselessly on to the bleak pierhead.'

RICHARD GORDON

JOHN Klaus Schneider, *Kirsten*'s captain, has a wiry build and a look of intense concentration which belies a wry sense of humour. I don't know if this accounted for his monosyllabic answers or if he was just being precise.

When he told me that his ship crosses the Irish Sea 300 times a year, I understood the lines around his eyes and his pallid complexion. These working boats are now virtually all manned by foreign captains – a couple of Germans but mainly Poles and Filipinos. The lack of English boats means you hardly ever get an English captain. As well as losing our boat-building tradition we seem to be giving up our Merchant Navy heritage.

Klaus' assertion that we would not be bothered by the rough seas proved correct. Looking way down from the bridge to the water crashing over the deck and the anonymous containers piled high, it seemed impossible that our passage was so gentle: a slight rocking motion fore and aft that was not much different from being at the bow of *Hirta* in a gentle swell. It made a pleasant change to have no responsibilities for the boat and I admired *Kirsten*'s sophisticated navigation gear, especially the radar and autopilot. I was amused, though, by the helm. *Hirta*'s heavy wooden wheel is a pleasingly solid effort about 3 feet across; *Kirsten*'s manual steering gear is a 6-inch joystick.

Liverpool, Irish Sea, Belfast, Bangor

SHIP'S LOG: GALE-FORCE WINDS,
SEA STATE VERY ROUGH.

JOHN Once past the Isle of Man we turned north, into the wind. The passage was rougher for a while but the sea had calmed and the sun was shining when I came back on deck just after six o'clock. Klaus manoeuvred the ship precisely and calmly against the dock wall in Belfast and, within minutes, cranes looking like enormous clockwork toys moved in and started unloading the containers.

We headed for Bangor, and Fealty's pub. I was sitting in the back of the taxi when the driver looked hard at me through the mirror.

'What's your name?' he asked.

'John McCarthy,' I replied.

He thought for a moment. 'I've been reading Brian Keenan's book.' He started chuckling. 'Shouldn't you be in the boot?'

SANDI The wind had dropped a little but not enough to release *Hirta* from Liverpool. I was bored and occupied myself about the boat. I fixed the frayed edges on the crown knot of the gate rope on the starboard side. I did such a splendid job of tightening it that it's become too short to use. It's good to see how useful I'm becoming. Pol scrubbed the deck with gusto.

'I expect John's having a really good time in Ireland,' he enthused, splashing water around him.

'Hrrmph!' I snorted. Bloody weather.

A docker strolled along and admired *Hirta*. I asked him about the boats moored around us. He shook his head in disgust.

'Big bastard behind you, been taking fish out of the Mersey before they spawn. Be no fish left soon. Gits. And that rust bucket over there –' I followed his gaze across the docks. '– Yugoslavian. Well, they were when they arrived. Crew's half whatcha-call-it Serbs and half Croats. Impounded months ago – some kind of financial trouble.'

'At least they've missed the war,' I said.

'True, true. Not happy, though. Can't sail, can't come ashore. Sixteen months. Still, don't want them claiming on the Social, do we?'

He wandered off. I walked past the decaying ship. The stranded crew lives in squalor, entirely dependent on local donations for food. Welcome to Europe.

It was kind of the city to hold the Lord Mayor's Parade on a day when I'd got nothing to do. In the heart of town I came across marching majorettes in green velveteen tops and tartan skirts. I once worked with Spike Milligan. During a rather serious rehearsal someone set off a yodelling tape and he began to weep with laughter, calling yodelling his 'comic Achilles heel'. I'm like that with majorettes. If I'm ever at death's door and they march a troop of baton-swingers through my ward, I'll be up in an instant.

The floats were great. I was especially fond of the Post Office which had decided the best way to advertise its wares was with a post van accompanied by a man doing karaoke, dressed as Elvis Presley. He sang 'Cheating Heart'. At least, I think that's what it was. A truck carrying wounded women caught my eye as they dripped past in blood and bandages, protesting about NHS cuts. I've never seen a political float in a parade before but in Liverpool you say what you like.

The Lord Mayor and Lady Mayoress seemed unperturbed and waved apolitically at everyone. Behind them some aged chap stood to attention in a Gilbert and Sullivan uniform. I don't know what he was. A Lieutenant-General of the county or some such thing. It seemed oddly archaic in such a modern city. Britain forges on and drags the past silently behind. I can't say it was a big turn-out. I suspect Liverpool would go about its business whatever was happening. Maybe the Royal Family should go and live there. I bet it would be left to get on with it. The Liverpool accent would make the Windsors seem so much jollier.

 I waited for Brian in Fealty's bar. As I started my second pint there was still no sign of him and I began having doubts. He is the best friend in the world but his plans are subject to sudden changes. Two days before his book was published

he'd gone sailing and ended up becalmed in the Bay of Biscay. Publishers and booksellers waited anxiously until the boy arrived, with minutes to spare, bemused by their concerns. He turned up now, bouncing jauntily into the bar, gave me a hug and demanded 'Where've you been?', the wicked gleam in his eye challenging me to take the bait. I resisted the temptation and explained how the weather had forced us to change our plans.

Brian Keenan in uncharacteristic pose.

He was disappointed to be missing Sandi but could not altogether hide his delight that our plans had been thwarted.

'That'll teach you,' he crowed. 'You Brits think you can go where you like. But that's the Irish Sea out there, Johnny, so you's best show it some respect.'

It's a joy talking to Brian. It is so easy to express yourself to someone who has shared so many intense experiences.

'So is the sailing as good as we thought it would be?' he asked eagerly.

'In many ways, yes, but we overlooked one simple but very important fact.'

'What's that?' he laughed.

'Small boats move around a hell of a lot more than we gave them credit for. It took me ages to get used to all the rolling about.'

'Tell me about it,' he said. 'On my jaunt to Biscay I spent a night trussed up in a tiny bunk, thinking: "This is like those godawful moves in Lebanon." Have you been frightened?'

'Yes, I have.'

We looked at each other steadily. When we first met it had taken a while to be able to admit our fears to each other; men aren't supposed to do that. Our friendship became too deep for foolish conventions and our survival through four years of shared incarceration was based on the ability to express our feelings openly and be prepared to admit, happily, that we needed each other's support. We never speak of fear lightly.

In captivity, one thought of physical freedom as being synonymous with freedom from fear and had not properly anticipated that fear would be an integral part of the reality of the great escape of sailing.

'So you've been frightened. Fine. But do you want to stop your journey?' he asked.

I thought for a moment. 'No, I want to keep on. Somehow my fears on the boat are liberating. They test you, then reward you with pure exhilaration.'

Earlier in the year I'd been over in Dublin to work on a film script Brian's writing about our captivity. It had been a great relief to find that we could work through the captive years so well together, happy to be making sense of it all and putting the experience further behind us. It was no surprise when he asked me: 'How's it going with so many of you on that wee boat? Any mutinies yet?'

'Not so far, but we're working on it!' I went on: 'Our fantasies of sailing were bloody ignorant but we were right about the joy of being able to get out of the confines of the cabin and go and stare away across the sea. You can lose yourself for a while there and then come back refreshed.'

'Aye,' he said, 'I can see that.'

He was over the moon at winning a bet we'd made in one of our cells. We'd designed our dream boat and Brian had been insistent on incorporating a coal stove. I'd said it would be impossible on a wooden boat. *Hirta* proves he was right.

As we talked, the bar filled up and the music began. Brian had told me of the 'sessions' at Fealty's long ago and it was a real pleasure to sit and enjoy it with him, his wife Audrey and some of their old friends from Belfast who were down for the night. It started as a very happy evening with the lively traditional music of pipes and fiddles enhancing the warm atmosphere I always experience when among Irish people. With every passing Guinness the evening became even more mellow.

SANDI We are to set sail for Scotland and John must make his way there as best he can. We shall have to get moving as the small window of favourable weather is not due to last for long. The journey ahead is a good 170 miles and it's going to take us the best part of some thirty-six hours, the longest we'll have been at sea in one go. I tried to shop but it's almost impossible to think ahead for thirty-six hours. The boat has no fridge or even cool-box to keep things fresh and your mind slips from vegetable selection to information scraps about scurvy. I headed down the aisles of ready-prepared food as all the forecasts are for conditions I would definitely describe as choppy.

DAY 23 Liverpool, Irish Sea, County Down

SHIP'S LOG: WINDS WEST-SOUTH-WESTERLY FORCE 6,
SEA STATE ROUGH.

SANDI You can't just sail out of Liverpool docks. You have to pass through a lock system in a complex rite of passage. Behind a Navy patrol boat, we passed acres of silent warehouses, their exteriors battered and abandoned as their giant insides wept from disuse. The sounds of a once-busy port seemed to echo in the air but there was little time to reflect. Once the heavy metal lock gates opened we could see substantial white caps forming on the Mersey. We turned upriver, seeking quieter waters to raise the mainsail before turning away from the city. It was blowing fairly hard and we settled down to a comfortable sail as we passed a shipwreck in the Channel. I looked the other way. After a few hours we could just see the Blackpool Tower in the distance. The Irish Sea stretched out ahead of us, its waters splashing across the bow preventing any sleep or relaxation. We resorted to eating tinned meat.

SWEET F A

This is the British sailors' name for tinned meat in the nineteenth century. Canned beef was introduced in 1813, the year after Sweet Fanny Adams, a well-known prostitute, was murdered. Her body was cut into pieces and thrown into the River Wey in Alton, Hampshire. Her name became synonymous with anything worthless.

JOHN I'd heard from Sandi that there was now no hope of *Hirta* making it across the Irish Sea to pick me up. The time loss would punish an increasingly tight schedule too much. Even if they leave Liverpool today they will take at least thirty-six hours to make landfall in Scotland, so I have time on my hands. I hope Sandi will be all right; we've become such a team I feel I'm letting her down badly by swanning around over here.

Brian and Audrey took me to a Gaelic football match at a county fair in Newcastle, County Down. Our route took us on the little car-ferry over Strangford Lough. Brian pointed out an old windmill, saying: 'Remember I told you about this derelict tower I'd wanted to buy and write poetry in, looking out over a lough?'

'Yes, you were going to be another W.B. Yeats, weren't you?'

'That's right, and that's the tower.'

I saw the two of us again, huddled on a mattress in the Beqa'a Valley, using pencil and paper to work out how to build a platform on the top of Brian's tower, using a fan of playing cards to visualize a spiral staircase.

We drove on through small, deserted fishing villages to Newcastle, set beside the sea at the foot of the Mourne Mountains which were half-hidden in mist. There was a large crowd to support teams from all over County Down and, behind the stadium, music and dance contests were in progress.

Brian knew little more than me about the rules. The men kicked, held and bounced the ball in a mixture of Association Football, rugby and basketball. As we watched we became more bewildered. A chap called Gerry sidled up and explained the rules at great length. Most of their intricacies went over our heads. At the end of the match the scores were equal, but one of the teams was declared a winner since it had come from further away to take part. We were asked to present the medals to the winners who hadn't won a game we hadn't understood. I am always happy to be in Ireland.

We all had to move on – Brian and Audrey back to Dublin, me somehow to meet up with *Hirta*. Our spur-of-the-moment decision to split up, and the unpredictable moods of the seas, had left us with no arrangements about how or where to meet up again. I had no luck with any of the contact numbers in Liverpool – they'd already left.

SANDI By 9.30 in the evening, Tom decided that he and I had already been off-watch for an hour and a half, which was news to me and everybody else. I was wearing long johns, track suit bottoms, my thermal trousers and my over-trousers, a polo-neck sweater, a thermal sweater, a proper sweater, a fleecy jacket

Crossing Morecambe bay.

and a waterproof jacket and was obviously dressed for a bit of a lie-down. The boat was thrashing about so by the time I'd stripped off, clenched my buttocks on to the toilet and tied my bed up with a series of unsuccessful clove hitches it was nearly time to get up again.

I didn't mind. My bedding gave new meaning to the concept of dampness as, indeed, did I. I was damp through to the pith of my being. Besides which, I was tired of holding on. The pipe cot is the only bed on board which doesn't have storm sheets to hold you in. It's also the only bed where you could fall from a substantial height. I wedged myself into a crevice and clung on to anything

Foreign, for'ard and fed up.

resembling a vertical position. Inches above my head the wooden jib and staysail blocks flamencoed with each other.

OLD SAYING

'He who would go to sea for amusement would go to hell for pleasure.'

ANON (verified Toksvig)

Midnight came before I knew it. Feeling grumpy and disorientated, I arrived on deck to find myself smiling. The Isle of Man was now on our port side and a surprising number of lights along the centre of the island were clearly visible. It made me feel good. We've spent so much time looking at nothing but sea that I felt heartened by the sight of a proper town with life going on as normal. Even if you can't actually see people going about their business, you need to know they're there.

There was a strange time during the night-watch when Tom went below a lot because he had to navigate. It was pouring with rain. I was alone before the mast – well, behind it, but alone on deck anyway – straining my stomach and leg muscles to keep my seat on the narrow cockpit ledge while still watching the compass. One violent gust of wind and I flew across the cockpit, spinning the wheel behind me. I realized I could quite happily tumble out of the boat and *Hirta* might be in Alaska before anybody was any the wiser. I was both unnerved and strangely intoxicated to be in sole charge of the old girl as the rain pounded through the night. There was a weird phosphorescent quality in the white tops of the waves as my eyes struggled to focus on the dusky orange glow of the compass rose. In the distance the comforting lighthouse at the end of the Isle of Man on the Point of Ayre beckoned me on.

THE ISLE OF MAN WRENS

Sailors used to believe that the feather of a wren, especially one killed on New Year's Day, would protect them from death by shipwreck. The feather's power only lasted for one year. The superstition led to the annihilation of the wren population on the Isle of Man. Lucky for the sailors, obviously not wildly lucky for the wrens. Still, a good-luck token preferable to the carrying of a caul, which was also popular. The caul is part of the amniotic sac which covers the head of a new-born baby. The caul was carried to prevent you drowning. I imagine it also prevented you being invited to many dinner parties.

At night, my basic theory is that all boats are coming straight for you. People may say 'That tanker's half a mile away' but I'm not confident. You're supposed to look for their port and starboard lights to see whether they're heading towards or away from you. There are various rules about it. I think it's 'green to green, red to red, all is safe, go ahead' – or something. All I could think of was 'red and green should never be seen' – but I think that's some kind of fashion tip passed on to me as a child and not really a useful navigational technique.

We were heading up past the Mull of Galloway – the rain had stopped messing about and was falling by the bathtubful. The breeze decided to play up and we had to rouse Pol to get the jib down. The large amount of canvas we were carrying was pressing the boat too hard. I realized that I can now feel when *Hirta* is happy and when she is not. A strange transformation from visitor to friend. Tom extended our watch by an hour. By 3 a.m. I was frozen and soaked. Fully-dressed, I crawled into my suspended bed, lashed myself to a hook and slept.

The voyage is a constant series of twists and turns between what you expect and what actually happens. I have to stop anticipating anything and just relax into the sea's own rhythm. Perhaps I am beginning to learn.

Belfast, Stranraer, Campbeltown, Isle of Arran

DAY 24

SHIP'S LOG: WINDS SOUTH-WESTERLY FORCE 6, SEA STATE ROUGH.

JOHN I discovered that *Hirta* sailed from Liverpool for Scotland yesterday, probably heading towards the Isle of Arran. The weather reports for the other side of the Irish Sea were not good and I hoped that there would be no serious difficulties for the team. Although I had an early start, there were no ropes to pull, just a ticket to buy.

I left Belfast for Stranraer in Scotland on a SeaCat ferry. Travelling at just under 40 knots, the passage took only ninety minutes. The sea appeared calm and I had hardly any sense of our speed over the water, but looking out at the stern the ship's massive engines were throwing up giant plumes of water. The captain tried to raise *Hirta* on the radio, but without success. I was pleased to see that the SeaCat had a steering wheel, not a joystick, but it looked as if it should be on a tiny motor car rather than a large ferry.

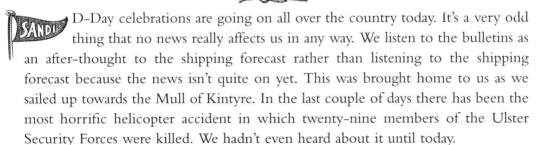

SANDI D-Day celebrations are going on all over the country today. It's a very odd thing that no news really affects us in any way. We listen to the bulletins as an after-thought to the shipping forecast rather than listening to the shipping forecast because the news isn't quite on yet. This was brought home to us as we sailed up towards the Mull of Kintyre. In the last couple of days there has been the most horrific helicopter accident in which twenty-nine members of the Ulster Security Forces were killed. We hadn't even heard about it until today.

Now we're coming up the eastern side of the Mull, heading for Campbeltown. I've been up since seven after four hours' sleep. The rain has eased a little and we're making good progress; the hills of Scotland are on our right. Pol has been taking compass bearings of landmarks and comparing them to the chart. I'm not sure I've got the hang of it.

'That thing on the hill.' Pol pointed to the shore. 'Do you think it's a radio mast or an old watch-tower?'

I peered through the drizzle. 'Looks like a 1950s petrol pump to me.'

It was unlikely and unhelpful.

We sailed in past the eastern side of a small island just beyond the mouth of Campbeltown Harbour. Up on the cliffs, a large white lighthouse with a couple of adjacent houses appeared abandoned. The velvety hills sloped steeply down towards the water where a large Navy warship was moored incongruously at a wooden jetty. Large, Gothic houses were dotted around the hills. If you want isolation this is clearly the place.

Mid-afternoon, mid-week, and Campbeltown was closed. I wandered amongst the deserted grey stone buildings in search of life. A local woman told me: 'Last weekend was the Bank Holiday for the rest of the world and today it is for Campbeltown'. Obviously a highly independently-minded small town. Outside the 1930s Victorian town hall, a home-made cut-out of a man roller-skating invited me to join in at 8.30 p.m. The man was wearing black with a red tie-belt so it was obviously a bit of a racy evening.

JOHN We made contact in Stranraer. *Hirta* was not far away but the north-easterly wind meant that she was in Campbeltown on Kintyre. They are still hoping to make Arran tomorrow so I'm going north by car to Ardrossan to catch a ferry over to the island to wait for them. I am enjoying driving again. It makes a pleasant change to be completely in control of a journey, understanding the road and the vehicle. Despite the high points on this trip there are so many times on *Hirta* when I feel quite out of my depth.

DAY 25 Campbeltown, Isle of Arran, Holy Island

SHIP'S LOG: GALE-FORCE WINDS FORECAST, SEA STATE VERY ROUGH.

SANDI I think it's a Monday. *Hirta*'s not going anywhere today. Having spoken to John we decided to spend an enforced non-sailing day on Arran.

The Loch Tarbert ferry is a larger version of the *King Harry* ferry. As it arrived, its front just flopped down on to the quayside so we could board for Lochranza on the Isle of Arran. I asked the captain what the main industry on Arran is now. 'Tourism,' he replied, to which I added 'and presumably sweaters'. He laughed. Turns out the sweaters are from a completely different Aran. I tore up my Christmas

POSTCARD NUMBER 6. *Isle of Arran, an unusual view of one of the most beautiful places in the British Isles.*

shopping list. I think it's very naughty of the UK to have so many places with the same name.

After a reunion hug with John we headed to Lamlash on the other side of Arran. We were hoping to get across to Holy Island, where we'd heard a new religious community had been founded. As we arrived, the weather was blowing up and a good deal of discussion ensued with Harold, the boatman who runs the small ferry across the bay. Harold is a Yorkshireman with a sailor's cap and moustache which makes him look like the archetypal ferryman.

We were slightly bewildered by our new skipper. Once he decided we could leave, he first rowed to a small motor boat and tied the row-boat to it. Then he took the small motor boat to a larger motor boat and transferred again. We had a notion that he was going to continuously go from one boat to a slightly larger boat all morning but he returned, ramming into the jetty.

JOHN When Sandi landed from the ferry she seemed in good spirits, but the tough thirty-two-hour sail from Liverpool had left her exhausted. Still, it was good to be together again. We caught up on news as we headed for the Buddhist retreat on Holy Island. The Samye Ling Tibetan Centre in Eskdalemuir bought the island just over two years ago. With the help of volunteers the monks are reaffirming the island's long spiritual history as a place of pilgrimage and contemplation, building a centre for Buddhist retreats and another complex for inter-faith gatherings.

As we approached the tiny jetty in the choppy swell we could see a number of monks walking along in saffron and maroon robes.

'I feel a bit nervous,' admitted Sandi.

I realized that I did too. 'How do you address a monk?' I asked.

Sandi shrugged. 'Don't know.'

'I hope they don't think we've just come to stare.'

Sandi looked at me. 'Haven't we?'

We passed down a roofless stone corridor to the smiling monks. I felt we were running a gauntlet as we approached them but they soon put us at ease with their smiling faces and the atmosphere of contentment they exude.

We were honoured with the presence of their principal teacher, Lama Yeshe Losal. Lama means teacher in Tibetan. Lama Yeshe outlined their plans for the island. He is a gentle man, bubbling over with a friendliness that encompasses all those around him. He told us that he'd dreamt about an island many years before and when he first came to Lamlash Bay he knew it was the same place and that he must build a monastery here.

Sandi, John, Lama Yeshe Losal (third from the left) *and a monk who's taken 283 vows of abstinence.*

SANDI The whole island is devoted to meditation. The Lama told us that meditation comes in stages. At the first level it is like a small stream and then it becomes more like a sea, until finally it is an ocean and you transcend the 'busyness of mind' which most Westerners are plagued by. The monks are untroubled by the notion of urgency. We admired a dry stone wall under construction – a 5-foot high arc of crafted rocks sweeping from the jetty to the farmhouse. The Lama said it's like a dragon spreading its way across the island. The monk in charge of building reckons the finished wall will take him another five years. Everyone seemed to think that was a perfectly sensible use of time. Five years. I even use instant mash when I'm cooking.

The farmhouse end, where we had arrived, is due to be turned into a general retreat for any member of the public. Inside, a shrine had been created with upturned orange boxes for prayer tables and 1960s life-jackets as cushions. The Lama says he can't swim. He will drown if it is his time. He lives surrounded by the sea and sits upon a life-jacket.

One monk told me he'd taken 283 separate vows of abstinence. I had no idea there was so much to give up.

 The conversation gave our voyage a new perspective. I spoke to one young monk, an Englishman, who had gone on a four-year, predominantly silent, retreat with Lama Yeshe. Having had a type of retreat forced on me I wondered what it was like to go by choice and if he had had any regrets. He said that the first year had been a difficult period of adjustment but, once through that, he had been able to focus on his prayer and study and benefit from it. I had shared some of this experience in captivity. After a year in shock I began to recognize myself more clearly in that harsh environment than ever before. I can appreciate that a benign, positive form of deprivation might be liberating for some, although I am wary of going into retreat by choice.

'Do you have any advice for our long journey?' Sandi asked the Lama as we said our goodbyes.

'Be of the moment,' smiled the Lama.

We left happy and refreshed.

DAY 26 East Loch Tarbert, Loch Fyne, Crinan

SHIP'S LOG: WINDS WESTERLY, FORCE 5.

I'm trying to be 'of the moment'. I'm not entirely sure how to do it. I think you have to appreciate the 'now' and not look backwards or forwards. We're chugging up Loch Fyne, home of the utterly splendid Loch Fyne oyster. Mist has settled on the hills covered in pine trees. It's hard to imagine what this part of Scotland looked like before the arrival of pines. They're not indigenous to the area.

They came only in the last half-century when forestation schemes became bizarre tax-avoidance dodges for the wealthy. They have changed the face of Scotland.

⁂

JOHN We encountered stiff breezes and some squally showers but the scenery was magnificent: shafts of sunlight illuminated the dark green hillsides revealing small communities of whitewashed cottages. A magnificent rainbow arched across the contrasts of light and dark. For us, it was wonderful passing such scenery. For the people over there, it's home. We move on too fast to comprehend their lives. There was a lot of laughter, which was good, and much talk of the glory of Loch Fyne oysters, which left me unimpressed. A few days ago I was encouraged to eat one and found myself nearly choking on a salty bit of rubber.

'There is nothing in Christianity or Buddhism that quite matches the sympathetic unselfishness of an oyster.'

SAKI

⁂

SANDI At Ardrishaig the sun came out and we joined the first ancient lock of the Crinan Canal. Once the water pumped us up to the correct level, the road bridge ahead was raised. The entire A83 came to a halt as we passed on sedately, heading for the Western Isles and some of the most spectacular scenery in Scotland.

But first there was a lot of shouting. A fairly substantial modern yacht had already entered the first lock and it was unclear from a distance whether there was going to be room for both of us. Tom did a lot of shouting, in which the word 'abort' featured heavily, but we didn't. The lock-keepers wisely went about their business.

CANAL FACTS

The 9-mile Crinan Canal runs across Argyll from Loch Fyne to the Sound of Jura, cutting out what would otherwise be a 120-mile journey around Kintyre for travellers from the Western Highlands to Glasgow. The canal was begun in 1793 and took the bulk of nine years to complete. It has eight locks going up to a height of 68 feet above sea level and then seven locks stepping back down again. In its heyday, 2000 passengers travelled by luxury paddle-steamer through the system. Now, we're the biggest thing around.

JOHN It seemed strange to be on *Hirta* on absolutely flat water with land only a few feet away on either side. It was stranger still to be looking up from the deck to the lock gates where the water was at eye-level, threatening to burst through and flood us.

OPPOSITE: *A view of the Crinan Hotel. You could hear the piano from here.*

 I took to my fold-up bicycle, a breath of fresh air and a minute to myself. How wonderful to be under my own power. Cycling ahead to hand-crank the giant sluice gates and let *Hirta* pass through, I've decided I like sailing in places where you have land on either side of the boat. You can choose to sail or walk or ride a bike as you pass some of the most invigorating scenery in the world. A small hailstorm had heralded our entrance to the canal but soon it subsided into rain and then a sunny and happy day.

It is utterly satisfying to lean your back against the huge wooden gates and feel it relax against the water. Malcolm, one of the lock-keepers, said there's quite a lot of arguing in the summer by the locks. It seems that, nearly always, men are in the boats steering and shouting at their wives whom they've made go ahead to open up the lock. I viewed the lads on our boat. At least no one was shouting.

In the heart of the canal you reach the summit of sea-level and look out across forest-hugged mini-lochs like some slice of my Scandinavian homeland. As we began our descent we could look ahead to the sea and the romance of the Western Isles.

We moored in a small basin at Crinan, before the last two locks that take you out to the sea. As usual, we were glad to arrive. Twice *Hirta* had touched bottom and Tom had got in a panic and prophesied leaks, eventual sinking and so on. The bottom was soft but occasionally people throw a fridge-freezer or some such into the canal and you can't always see it. Sailing is all about hidden dangers.

By the end of the day we had been through twelve locks and, although exhausted, I was delighted to have mastered heaving the heavy ropes up on to the lock sides. Malcolm said he loathes all the big cities he's visited, preferring the peace and friendliness of Western Scotland. I understand. From the moment I saw Loch Crinan I felt I'd found somewhere I could live.

In the Crinan Hotel an earnest boy played the piano, vigorously depressing the loud pedal and most of the guests. A smart woman in pearls became agitated and then frantic, shouting at him: 'I've fractured my skull. You don't understand. It's very painful to listen to.' You don't often get such good outbursts in smart hotels. I rather enjoyed it. It really works as a line if you're not keen on the pianist.

DAY 27 Crinan

Still here.

DAY 28 — Crinan

SANDI It's my brother's birthday and I think it's Thursday. However, I have become 'sea sensitive' and could spot the instant I donned my oilskins that we weren't going anywhere in an open boat. Bad weather, you see.

An engineer has been called to look at *Hirta*'s starter motor. 'How is she?' I asked him. 'Old,' he replied.

In the evening I arranged a Scottish dinner for us all followed by a *ceilidh*. After haggis and neeps, a couple in fine voice and fettle sang Tracy Chapman songs on the guitar. It wasn't perhaps as Scottish as I had hoped.

HAGGIS

A Scottish dish consisting of a mixture of the minced heart, lungs and liver of a sheep or calf mixed with suet, onions, oatmeal and seasonings and boiled in the stomach of the slaughtered animal. Odd that it's so tasty.

DAY 29 — The Garvellachs

JOHN The weather was still not up to sailing onwards, so what better than to set to sea in an even smaller boat than *Hirta* to visit some more islands with Lachlan MacLachlan, lighthouse-keeper to the Garvellachs. The 'Isles of the Sea' are a group of quite small and unoccupied islands in the Firth of Lorn. Lachlan picked us up in a small blue fishing boat called the *Cardaline*. It looked like a toy as it sped towards us with the tide. Lachlan is a small, extremely gentle man in his fifties perhaps, with a soft, throaty voice and a most curious old-fashioned beard.

SANDI Last night's spicy haggis was having its revenge and all I could think about was whether there would be a loo on board. There wasn't.

JOHN Lachlan, being a fisherman, knows the waters like the back of his hand, which was reassuring as we set off against the fierce tide. He steered a complicated course across the currents, at times manoeuvring within 6 feet of the

rocks. As we passed the island of Fladda we could see our first lighthouse painted brilliant white, standing keeper of safety for these waters.

SANDI Gaelic names streamed past our boat. Eilean is Gaelic for island. Across choppy waters lay Eileach an Naoimh – Island of the Saints – with its own small lighthouse and ancient chapel. Beyond are the islands of Jura, Mull and, somewhere in the low visibility, Colonsay. Magnificent. The Garvellachs themselves, almost treeless with craggy rocks, rise up above you with grass knots clinging on for survival. The only residents these days are sheep. On a number of the islands farmers simply deposit the sheep to fend for themselves. They come out a week or two in the year to bring the lambs off and tidy up any of the sheep who haven't quite made it. One of the islands was bought for five thousand pounds by a man who lives in a council house in Hendon. He uses it occasionally for very, very quiet holidays. I'd like to own an island.

JOHN Lachlan goes out to Eileach an Naoimh once a month to check everything's all right. Still reeling from Sandi's Scottish supper, I was regretting that we had agreed to help him. Lachlan took us ashore in a dinghy. This was not as straightforward as it sounds as there is no jetty. Just rocks. We were under strict instructions to step off the boat during an upswing motion and then keep climbing up the rocks in order to avoid the boat crushing our ankles. Lachlan drove the boat straight up to the rocks and I stepped ashore. It seemed simple but when I turned around the boat had dropped away 10 feet below me, exposing an expanse of cliff.

SANDI John was butch and leapt off first. It looked graceful. I followed but in a vengeful swell, and landed on top of him. The Nureyev and Fonteyn of ship-to-shore. I liked Lachlan's attitude to boating. His method of simply running the bow of his boat up on to the rocks worked well until our cameraman got in the way and became the only man I've ever seen to be run over by a boat on dry land.

JOHN We were safe – for the moment. The thought that the mild-mannered Lachlan might just be off his rocker flickered through my mind. Nevertheless we followed him across the island through thick bog grass and wild cotton plants. Lachlan kept to a sheep track to take us half a mile to the lighthouse. It was a steepish climb up to the platform. I only just stopped in time as the land abruptly dropped away 200 feet to the waves crashing on the rocks below.

OPPOSITE: *Mr Rugged.*

ALL IN A DAY'S WORK

Our loved ones:
'What did you do at work today?'

John and Sandi:
'We painted a lighthouse.'

SANDI The lighthouse was surprisingly small. More like one you might build for the kids. A ladder in the cliff-face led up to an octagonal platform. Here a small light with a store-cupboard was ready to protect all shipping. Below us, sheer rock was being pounded by the sea. John, Lachlan and I set to work in close quarters painting the lighthouse. One more person and we could have held hands and danced our way around it. The light is surprisingly simple. Just one camping-gas bottle releasing a jet of gas into a tiny bulb every six seconds. It's the fantastically thick, prismed glass around the bulb which makes it shine for such a distance. It doesn't seem possible close-up.

We scraped guano off the windows and whitewashed away rust spots. It's a peaceful occupation, slapping emulsion on while the mists swirl across the waters teasing the eye with glimpses of the Western Isles.

The lighthouse sparkled. My stomach did not. It was a tortured place. I tried to hide behind a rock to relieve the siege but slipped on a large pile of sheep dung instead. I was jealous of the sheep and filled with the glamour of show business.

After everyone had had lunch and I'd got rid of some of last night's dinner, we moved down to the other end of the island. The now-deserted island was once occupied for generations and the ruins of ancient buildings stand abandoned. A beehive cell, built by Irish monks in the sixth and seventh centuries, still looks as though you might pass a fairly snug night in it. The walls, perhaps some 4 or 5 feet thick, are of slate, the only building material available on the virtually treeless island.

John and I stood inside looking out to sea through the narrow window slits.

'You'd have to be a very dedicated monk to think that this was a good idea,' John said thoughtfully.

I shared my guidebook reading with him. 'St Columba is supposed to have received a vision here from an angel with a glass bible telling him who was to be the next king.'

'A couple of months of this and you'd be imagining anything.'

Further on, a tenth- or eleventh-century monastery had stood the test of time even if the monks hadn't. The dry-stone walling technique was so good it almost looked like stone cladding rather than the real thing.

GAS ORDER
FOR A SMALL LIGHTHOUSE

About six bottles a year.

JOHN The sea was calm but it was a cloudy day and the islands around us looked primeval, like the ragged teeth of a colossal dinosaur.

'Don't want to be out here in bad weather,' said Lachlan as he pointed out the island's freshwater spring. 'I was christened from that. All the MacLachlans are.'

'Do you feel it's your island?' I asked him.

He scratched his beard. 'Well, my great-great-grandfather was born here and my father and grandfather before me looked after the lighthouses but we don't own it. It's owned by one of the law Lords. He has a moustache and a shooting bonnet and he comes here and he's clearly the lord.' Sandi kicked a turf in disgust.

The area is perfect for lobster fishing. On the way back from the Garvellachs we stopped to inspect a couple of Lachlan's creels. I hauled up two pots from a depth of some 30 feet. Just the thought of doing this often and in bad weather was exhausting. The second pot was complete with two residents, curious creatures with a really blue hue to their black shells. Sandi eyed them.

'You can hypnotize lobsters, you know. If you rub the hardest part of their backs it puts them to sleep.' I declined to have a go but she continued anyway: 'There was a head-waiter in Pennsylvania who could also get lobsters to do routines with two miniature paper umbrellas and a back flip, but that's probably best left to the experts.'

How does she know these things?

SANDI As we headed back, a group of a dozen seals lay sunning themselves on the rocks. Lachlan drove his boat close in to the thrashing waters. It was all 'Nae bother' and all pleasure. Most of the seals decided to push off as soon as they saw us, apart from one who solidly sat staring at these strange people with their strange cameras. He looked like Clive James on a bad day.

JOHN On the return journey Lachlan spoke with great affection about living and working among these desolate islands. He had hoped his son would take over as the fourth-generation lighthouse-keeper but everything is changing. Even the fishing life is under threat. The lack of fish in the area means his son has had to take the family trawler to Aberdeen hoping for better luck. Lachlan fears that with full integration of the EEC, Britain's over-fished waters will become dominated by foreigners. He surveyed the sea for a while, then said 'Ah, well, you've got to be philosophical about it and hope that something will work out. Try and make the best of things.' I think he would get on well with Lama Yeshe.

LOBSTERS

Here's a good word – benthic. It means bottom-dwellers. Lobsters are benthic. They also have poor social graces. They have one claw bigger than the other because they use the larger one for crushing and the smaller one for holding whatever's being crushed. The larger claw isn't always on the same side. Perhaps they are left- or right-handed like us. When a lobster outgrows its shell it eventually bursts out and leaves the entire thing behind. During this time, for about a month, it's fairly soft and vulnerable. This is a dodgy time because lobsters are a pretty mean bunch. If no crab or other creature happens past at lunchtime they are quite happy to eat each other. I imagine there's a fair old amount of trouble among the various benthic families. 'Larry! Have you eaten Uncle Albert?'

DAY 30

Firth of Lorn to Tobermory

SHIP'S LOG: WINDS WESTERLY FORCE 5 TO 6, SEA STATE MODERATE.

JOHN Off to Tobermory. Across the Firth of Lorn and then up the Sound of Mull, keeping the Island of Mull on our left and the Highlands on our right. We were approaching the Sound of Mull in perfect conditions when a band of fog appeared, obscuring it completely. Before the fog fell we had seen a number of ships about and we knew that some dangerous rocks, or bricks as Tom often calls them, were now hidden, so he warned us that we might have to change course for Oban. We ploughed on, straining for sight of anything in our path. There was a sense of fear in professionals and amateur sailors alike. Fortunately, almost as quickly as it had fallen the fog lifted. We sailed on, looking across to the Appin coastline.

We are all beginning to focus on the possibility of sailing out to Britain's most westerly inhabited islands, St Kilda. It would involve a major passage out into the Atlantic in notoriously dangerous seas. We will be very lucky to get the right conditions but, as *Hirta* is

OPPOSITE:
Hirta on starboard tack.

106

named after the main island of the St Kilda group, there would be great satisfaction in getting there. Originally, *Hirta* was called *Cornubia* after her home-county of Cornwall where she was built. It was the Marquis of Bute, owner of the St Kilda islands, who changed her name.

THE STEWARTS OF APPIN

Fine women. Centuries ago it was like this. The Stewart men had gone off to fight one of the other clans – the MacDonalds or whatever – but a fog arose and the men missed each other. Unchallenged, the enemy arrived at the Stewarts' homeland so the unprotected women of Appin put stones in their stockings, twirled them above their heads and commenced battle. They won what is now known as The Battle of the Stocking.

SANDI John and I had asked if we could perhaps take on more responsibility as crew and, actually having been given that responsibility, we found that we knew rather more than we thought. It was good to stand on the foredeck and not panic about which rope was which. Knowing that I was the one who had to go for the right rope, I actually did go for it. I think John's finding the same but we're both still learning.

Just when you think you're starting to get the hang of this navigation lark you learn of the desperate trickery the compass has been playing on you. The actual location of the geographical North Pole, and where your compass tells you it is, varies according to where you are in the world. It's called the magnetic difference. Around here it's 8 degrees west. You have to keep saying 'West is best and east is least': add the difference in the west and subtract it in the east. I knew I should have paid more attention to maths at school.

As we sailed into Tobermory we were allowed to stow the staysail on our own – a very simple task but new to us. It inspired a great feeling of unity and tremendous satisfaction. We both wanted to stand either side of it and have our photograph taken. We've been saying that one of the unexpected things we've learnt is that a lot of sailing is really simple if you can just relax. You have to forget jargon and try to be in tune with what's happening. Be of the moment, I guess. Feel the wind on your face and you find you've corrected the steering without thinking about it. Behind us Ben Nevis stood capped with snow; a great glacial fell reminded us of the transience of our presence.

DAY 31 Tobermory

The capital of Mull. It takes its name from the ancient and long vanished Tobar Mhoire, Gaelic for the Chapel of the Well of Mary. The present town dates from the 1780s when the British Society for Encouraging Fisheries decided to found a port in this wonderful, natural harbour. Today, Tobermory is one of those picturesque little fishing villages which feature heavily on stocking-filler calendars. From a distance the coloured houses along the front bespeak a way of village life now forever crystallized in the past. Up close it's a different matter. Most of the proper shops – such as the butcher's and the baker's – have closed down. In their place is the tourist bargain and the land of the tartan air-freshener. It is no longer a place where people simply live their daily lives. The town relies on outside money.

The sun had come out slightly and two men were busy painting one of the local inns, transforming it from white into a lovely dark blue at a great pace. It was as though the scenery was changing before our very eyes as we walked along the quayside. The wooden Tobermory fishing boats have an exceptionally pleasant shape. Rather a solid, comfortable middle and a very strong bow, like some fantastic matron of the seas who will allow no waters to stand in her way. They were surprisingly clean and tidy for fishing boats. Prawns are the main catch, along with something called squat lobster which I've never heard of but is apparently a key ingredient in scampi and chips. I suppose squat lobster and chips doesn't have quite the same ring to it.

Two fishers of prawns stood on the quay sorting out piles and piles of blue rope that had been sitting knitting itself into a jumper all winter. Cross chaps, prawn fishermen. Well, the price of prawns ain't what it ought to be. It seems the fishermen, who've gone to all the bother of catching the little wrigglers, receive one pound per pound of prawns, and immediately the fishmongers sell them for five pounds per pound having done absolutely nothing to them. Not so much as a wash and spruce up. The fishermen's boats, the *Dawn Treader* and the *Jacobite*, lay freshly painted and much-loved by the water's edge. The chap who built them with his son is now unemployed simply because nobody can afford these magnificent wooden-hulled, clinker-built fishing boats. What a waste. They said that they have three seasons in Tobermory – April, May and winter. If they get three weeks of

sunshine then they have had an extremely good and exceptional summer.

A strong yeasty smell leads you by the nose through the town like some old-fashioned Bisto kid. You could find Tobermory's whisky distillery blindfolded. John immediately fell into conversation with an old lady. Everyone confides in him. He is the adopted son of the nation.

JOHN At the distillery an elderly lady was buying some souvenirs. 'Christmas presents for my family,' she confided. 'Do you want to see a picture of my husband?' She pulled out a black and white photograph of a man in an old-fashioned Scout Master's uniform with the wide-brimmed hat. 'He died last year – such a nice man, I do miss him.' She paid for her presents and went off, anxious that 'my friend will be worrying about me'.

SANDI Alan, the distillery manager, arrived to give us the full tour. It's quite a business with lots of boiling, mashing and storing. In Scotland it's five years before the stuff is ready for tasting. Fortunately they've been making tipples in Tobermory for some time. After the tour we had a wee dram to be polite. And then another. Strong stuff. Probably best in your coffee but it made us happy. After the first drink I remembered an old quote: 'A torchlight procession marching down your throat'. After the second, I couldn't remember who said it.

JOHN We left clutching two bottles of their finest malt to have on the boat. It is surprising how accommodating and generous people have been to us when we turn up unannounced to disrupt their routines.

SANDI At a small shop on the harbour front, we bought some prawn sandwiches for lunch. In the heart of the prawn world we were served something miniature, tasteless, previously frozen and most likely Icelandic. What's wrong with this country and its taste-buds? I could almost hear Rick Stein weeping.

SHOPPING TIP
**You can buy warm vests
in any clothing shop in Scotland in June.**

OPPOSITE: *Tobermory, Isle of Mull.*

DAY 32

Tobermory to Eigg

SHIP'S LOG: WINDS WESTERLY FORCE 6, SEA STATE ROUGH.
COLD FRONT APPROACHING BRINGING UNSETTLED WEATHER.

JOHN We left Tobermory at 6.30 this morning with a good breeze for our passage to the island of Eigg. My hands and arms ached badly after hauling up the mainsail and setting the foresails. Sandi complained of the same thing and we decided we should do a few warm-up exercises before we start each day.

SANDI We pushed our way out, avoiding Calve Island, to pass Auliston Point and Rubha nan Gall. (Rubha is Gaelic for headland. It all becomes clear.) Britain is awash with islands. I had no idea. Scottish history pulsed around us as we passed the point called Maclean's Nose and Bloody Bay. Looking towards Ardnamurchan, you could just see the remains of Kilchoan Castle by Kilchoan Bay, with ivy clambering over the walls. Along towards Loch Sunart, I had a really strong sense of the glacial history of this area, with sharp fjords and mountains rising on either side of us. Ahead lay the Inner Hebrides.

THE INNER HEBRIDES

The islands of Coll and Tiree have a sad and shameful past. In the beginning of the nineteenth century the inhabitants were moved wholesale off the islands and many of them transported to Newfoundland. The islands are now occupied again but it seems that, for a while, sheep made a better proposition for the landlords than annoying locals. Apparently there are parts of Nova Scotia where Gaelic is still spoken. Tiree, which is so flat it appears like a brushstroke on the horizon, means Land of Corn. It certainly isn't land of trees. No tree could stand up to the 120-knot winds which blow in off the Atlantic each winter. It is said you can tell people who come from Tiree because they're always standing at an angle.

JOHN The wind hardened and we were soon crashing through the waves towards the Ardnamurchan peninsula on the mainland when a squall hit us, driving rain into our faces. We were prepared and in our oilskins; a few weeks ago this would have been a preoccupying concern for us, now it's become routine. The landscape around is beautiful; rock-covered, low-lying hills with sheep grazing all around. Twenty minutes later we rounded the Point of Ardnamurchan, the westernmost tip of mainland Britain.

We had to keep well off from the Point, a dangerous area, and endured what Tom and Pol call 'square' waves; large blocks of water coming from all directions caused by the tide churning over a submerged ledge of rock as it meets the incoming swell of the Atlantic. *Hirta* pushed on through the waves, well heeled-over, with water running down the lee side of the deck and waves occasionally breaking over the bows. I was at the helm for a while and although, at times, still apprehensive that we would capsize as a gust of wind hit us, deep down I knew we were safe and could concentrate on keeping the boat sailing fast to windward. Tom said this was a millpond compared to the seas we might meet if we head out west to St Kilda. I think I will worry about that when it happens.

At last we could begin to make out the shapes of different islands. First of all the small island of Muck; beyond that our destination, Eigg; and most prominent of all, the island of Rhum. *Hirta* leapt to her fastest as we heeled over to new flights of daring. Steering was a challenge. Every now and then she wanted to lift her stern up out of the water and you had to anticipate it and steer against it. It was the now familiar combination of fear and fun.

Just outside the southern harbour of Eigg, a small island – Eilean Chathastail – stood sentry. You can pass up a small channel beside it into the harbour but this was deemed too dodgy. We went round where there are lots of reefs. Rock and a hard place job, really. Before we left *Hirta* it was decided this would be a two-pants stay, which means nobody knows how long we'll be here.

The west wind was blowing straight into the anchorage at the south end of Eigg where we had planned to moor *Hirta*, so Tom dropped us off and went on with Pol to find a quieter mooring off Canna. We landed at the quay at Galmisdale and wandered up to eat in the café. David Robertson, a very fit-looking young man with short brown hair and an open, forthright manner, turned up in his clapped-out van to transport us across the island. All the B & B accommodation was full but he had a caravan we might be able to use.

Originally from Glasgow, David moved here to run his wife's family croft. They have a permanent tenancy all the while it stays in the family. As we drove across the island David pointed out the school, which has eleven pupils, and the store. This corrugated-iron building, set against a deserted landscape of heather and bracken-covered hills, brought to mind images of frontier communities.

Abandoned old cars are everywhere. When they conk out they're left, and get broken up by anyone who can find a useful spare part. There is no regular refuse collection; just a clear-up every two or three years. They burn what they can and bury the rest or pile it up. David and his neighbours, aside from their physical separation, really are living on the edge of our society.

There is no mains electricity on Eigg so everyone has a bank of batteries and a generator. No one runs theirs for twenty-four hours a day so the island has a large communal freezer room for everyone's frozen provisions. It's run on an honesty policy with the doors left open and people simply taking their own food. A while ago they found two campers stealing a cheesecake and some meat, and a padlock was put on the door, but everybody kept losing their keys so now it's open again. The cost of having meat brought over by ferry from the mainland is high so there are a lot of vegetarians.

Our caravan accommodation stood in a field below the giant rock face of the Scoraig, the heart of the island which rises up majestically in the centre – an

John outside the de luxe accommodation on Eigg.

114

extraordinary display of sheer granite with a pitted front to it. It was a little like being down in the Grand Canyon apart from the fact that it was cold and windy and we were in a field with a caravan. I've never slept in a caravan before. This one's a Venus De Luxe but not so de luxe that we can actually fit six of us in it. There's a wooden shed built on the side of it. It's obviously a caravan not destined for moving.

David invited us to a *ceilidh* at Maggie and Wes's. There are seventy-three people living on the island. I got the impression that most of them were going. Our party hosts lived in a stone house with the minimum of mod cons. Lit only by two hissing gas lamps swinging in the wooden rafters, the whole of the downstairs is one large room. In the centre of the room is a large, square, very old wooden table and a battered sofa covered in an old quilt, facing a Danish pot-bellied stove. Guests arrived with whatever drink they had. The island shop had run out of beer. We'd bought the last twelve-pack and people were bringing cans of cider and half-empty half-bottles of vodka.

Pretty soon somebody got a guitar out and then a woman began playing the accordion. It was traditional, lilting, Scottish/Irish folk music in which I always find it impossible to discern whether one tune is different from the last. It didn't matter. The focus was on the chat.

At the centre table, all the women dominated. They sat talking only to each other while a variety of children climbed over and under them, receiving varying degrees of attention. The men formed an outer ring, standing around the edge of the room, drinking as fast as they could, and as much as they could, of other people's drink. Like a Jewish wedding, it seemed impossible for John and I to do anything but join the group of our own sex.

JOHN Amongst the men, the island's absentee landlord Schellenberg, or Schelly as they call him, was the main topic of conversation. David had shown us the foundations for a new house he is building. Work has come to a halt while he waits for the landlord's permission to continue. Mr Schellenberg bought the island twenty years ago with high hopes of bringing economic stability and development to the community. None of his money-making schemes took off and there is now much resentment among the inhabitants against the man who they see as holding them back from self-sufficiency. They are now raising the money to try to buy the island.

SANDI While the men roared around us, the women talked in a way that I had almost forgotten about. I sat with Sheena, who runs the tea shop, and her friend Marie. Just two weeks before, Sheena's eleven-year-old son Alexander had died in a tragic accident. He and two friends had been playing with some rope when he accidentally hanged himself. The whole island was in shock. Sheena, the dark circles of grief under her eyes stark in the gas light, talked freely to me, a stranger, about the support of the women on the island, about the great pains she could feel in her womb and about what an island community really means. Behind me the men became drunker and drunker while the music played.

 More people arrived, some of the men already the worse for drink. The vet had been over from the mainland to tend to their sheep and it was a tradition to have a few drams with him. The drink flowed freely. But despite the lively music, the banter and the children playing around our feet, I detected a strong sense of sadness buried deep in this community, a compression of despair that spoke of tensions born out of the demands of survival. It's too early to tell how their struggle to gain independence will go and how well they would cope with sharing the responsibility of running the whole island; but I believe they have the will to succeed. They certainly deserve to.

As we were leaving a young scallop-diver took me by the arm. A handsome lad, he nodded towards John at the other side of room.

'I've been reading your friend John's book.'

'Oh, yes,' I replied.

'It's very good.'

I nodded. 'Yes. Yes, it is.'

'The trouble is,' he confided, 'I'm only two-thirds of the way through it. I don't know how it finishes.'

'Oh.' I tried to be soothing. 'Well, don't worry, he gets out in the end.'

'Oh, good,' said the diver, and went back to his drink.

 Eigg and Muck

I don't think caravanning is for me. I slept one end, while my technical boys slept the other and John had a mattress on the floor in the shed extension. The loo was behind a single piece of curtain by John's head. I don't know who had a more interesting time in the night as I stepped over his face in the dark to be excused. We were all a touch 'post-*ceilidh*'. It was probably a good time to have medical assistance around for the day.

I've met doctors before but never one who starts the day sucking his body into a rubber immersion suit. John and I don't have one of these so we suspected that a ducking was in the offing. We donned our Henry Lloyd sailing jackets and boarded a large, rigid inflatable with the kind of engines on the back which make James Bond smile. Chris Tiarks is a doctor in a 'designated special practice' and his tax-deductible boat is the only way he can get to his patients. He pulled an SAS-style balaclava over his head and climbed on the motor cycle seat behind the steering wheel. No illness would dare get in his way. We appeared to have set to sea on a bouncy castle during a violent storm.

JOHN Going at some 30 knots over a heavy swell in a small boat is an alarming experience. We held on with white knuckles, certain that if we let go for a moment we would fly out into the cold sea. Attempting to hold on, we landed in a heap of tangled legs and arms. Sandi and I were roaring with laughter that was only just this side of real hysteria. Occasionally Chris would turn to ask if we were OK and we would dutifully reply in the British manner, 'Fine, thank you, Chris; splendid,' and then hang on even tighter.

Muck is much smaller and more low-lying than Eigg. We came up to the little harbour in Port Mor and tied up to the quay. Muck is a tiny place, about 1 mile by 2 miles, with just under thirty residents. The bulk of the houses are concentrated at the small, stone pier where we landed. We sloshed up to the first house to make the first house-call where Chris changed out of his wetsuit.

Inside her corrugated bothy overlooking the harbour, Chris examined a wound on eighty-four-year-old Jessie's leg. Chris had been unable to visit Jessie for three weeks in January when the island had been storm-bound. Her legs had become ulcerated so she'd been flown by helicopter for six months' hospital treatment at Fort William, and the wounds were still healing. Her hands crippled with arthritis, she spends her days watching the island's comings and goings.

Chris's visit meant a lot to Jessie. Nowadays there is no priest or policeman on Muck and, aside from medical duties, Chris feels the doctor's role is very important in maintaining the focus of the people and regular links between the islands. He clearly values the traditional way of life the islanders are trying to preserve but knows that the apparent costs of it are anathema to the present Tory Government.

Muck exudes a great sense of togetherness.

Chris said he finds the people on Muck more contented than their neighbours and it occurred to me that this might be due to the difference in landlords. Muck's owner, Lawrence MacEwan, and his wife live and farm on the island and are an integral part of the community.

ABOVE: *Dr Chris Tiarks on his rounds.*
OPPOSITE: *The Fred and Ginger of seafaring arrive on Muck.*

Originally from Surrey, Chris is a highly politicized doctor with a passion for the notion of community and a concern for the vulnerability imposed on his island practice by the NHS reforms. He is responsible for the whole Small Isles community – Eigg, Muck, Rhum and Canna – and fears that once he retires the practice may go to a mainland doctor and then there would be no more routine visits. Cases like Jessie's, for example, would always become emergencies and not just in bad weather.

Individual attention for their children is something people pay a lot of money to public schools for. On Muck it's free. Barbara, the island teacher, has four children

in her charge – three boys from the Smith family and one girl, Mary, who's twelve. Everyone on Muck is delighted that the Smith family have come to the island. There was a time when Mary was the only child in the school, which must have made competitive sports a bit tricky. Soon three more children will be joining them and the school will be linked by computer to the other island schools.

Chris borrowed Barbara's truck to get him the mile over the other side of the island to see a crofter. Barbara was unsure if this was sensible: 'I trust you with my life,' she said. 'I'm not sure I trust you with my truck'.

NAPOLEONIC MUCK

The island did rather well in the Napoleonic Wars. The islanders used to burn seaweed in order to make potash, which is one of the primary components of gunpowder. It's a very odd notion that you could gather a bunch of old seaweed on Muck and end up killing somebody at the Battle of Waterloo.

DAY 34 Eigg

Shopping is a cinch on Eigg because there's only the one shop. The post had arrived when we got back. It comes in three times a week and turns the shop, a tiny corrugated affair stuffed with a bit of everything, into a magnet for the community. Fiona, who I'd met at the *ceilidh*, was busy behind the counter selling beer, tobacco, stamps, basics, whatever, while a group of kids hawked raffle tickets for a school trip.

There are no newspapers on Eigg. There's no point in them. Island news travels very fast by word of mouth and anything else is mainly irrelevant. Even if the islanders bothered to have them delivered, by the time the papers arrived the news would be so old as to be absurd. The effect is remarkable. You find yourself in a society where they don't know or care about the latest soap-star scandal or parliamentary indiscretion. The result seems to be a focusing on the community and its daily struggle with the vagaries of life. I found I was having philosophical discussions with complete strangers and making a strong, instant connection with women like Sheena. I think this is healthy and have begun to wonder at the mainland's obsession with newspapers which are not about news, don't help anybody and portray British life as a circle of scandal, sex and sleaze.

DAY 35 Eigg to Barra

JOHN Tom was in touch this morning by radio to say he thought there was a window in the weather to allow us to get to Barra in the Outer Hebrides, the best jumping-off point for St Kilda. We are all keen to try the proper ocean, but the weather pattern is so confused that it is impossible to predict what will happen next. Although we have not had any severe storms in these waters the winds have been variable to say the least and the sea is unsettled.

SANDI Before we left I asked David to take me up to the cemetery. I needed to say goodbye to the young boy I'd never met but whose lost life was so imprinted on my mind. The cemetery stands on a hill overlooking a small bay and out to Ardnamurchan. It's a ramshackle sort of place but the islanders have their own way of organizing it. The Protestants lie at the bottom of the hill, the Catholics at the top and over the brow of the hill, to one side, are the unconfirmed Catholics. Here lay Sheena's son, Alexander. The view was astounding and would have raised the depressed spirits of an atheist at the Second Coming. I missed my family.

JOHN The tragedy has devastated Eigg, yet, as an outsider, I felt that the way in which the islanders are sharing their grief and giving support to Alexander's family is an example that the wider community of Britain would do well to follow.

Farewell to Eigg.

SANDI A launch took us to reunite with *Hirta* by Hyskeir lighthouse on an island called Hyskeir. The *Frangang* was the way to zip round the country. Incredibly expensive and fast. We sped past Rhum and Canna and up to Hyskeir in one-third of the time *Hirta* would take.

There's a wrong and a right side to an island if you're approaching by inflatable. We chose the wrong side.

JOHN We scrambled up several hewn stone steps and floundered our way through long grass until we got to some rocks. The lighthouse stood massive at the far end of the island. Scores of terns dived and screeched angrily all around us. The head keeper, Jim, and his colleague Bill came to meet us half-way across and explained that the terns' eggs were nestled in little rock crevices all around us. We moved off quickly to leave the birds in peace. We followed the keepers gingerly along the narrow tracks through the grass and over sturdy iron bridges spanning rocks exposed by the low tide. Everything on Hyskeir is extremely solid and functional. It needs to be. The flat island is at the mercy of the elements.

Bill went ahead to send the hourly weather report to his colleagues in Tiree. It was a moment of revelation – these men are at the sharp end of the shipping forecast of which we are now devoted listeners.

LIGHTHOUSES

They often stand on sandreefs and mudflats where it is impossible to find a firm foundation. They are secured by means of the screw pile – a brilliant engineering device invented in 1832 by Irishman Alexander Mitchell, who was totally blind. The Seven Wonders of the World included a lighthouse – the Pharos lighthouse at Alexandria.

SANDI The lighthouse towered above us as we chatted with the men – Jim, a lighthouse-keeper for thirty years; Bill, a shy quiet man with a moustache; and David, a Max Wall figure in charge of cooking. These three keepers are among the last eleven manned-lighthouse teams in the country. Jim's been told he needs to lose weight but as Hyskeir is one of the tallest lighthouses in the country, he's doing that just by going up and down the stairs.

David showed me the month's menu which included his specialities of Spaghetti *à la* Hyskeir and Seagull Curry. He refused to reveal what was in Seagull Curry but offered up freshly-made Scottish pancakes, scones, Rice Krispies covered in chocolate and cups of tea. David showed off his freezer of food in their communal house at the foot of the tower. Anything fresh is at a premium as the relief helicopter only brings supplies twice a month. The men have their own vegetable garden and, with the help of a secret seaweed mulch, grow some of the largest vegetables in the UK. David had a turnip the size of a St Bernard's head and a carrot so large it was hard to look it in the eye.

JOHN The keepers' quarters were incredibly neat. Having come from rubbish-strewn Eigg it was a great contrast. But, unlike Eigg, it all seemed very utilitarian and I got no sense of the men making the place into a home.

Each man has his own miniature bunk-room and they share a small square lounge. In a room devoid of decoration, three high-backed chairs with wooden arms stood in a row facing the television.

SANDI At the front of the lighthouse, a clipped lawn appeared to be ready for an impromptu tea-party. It seemed absurdly neat and tidy. Usually it's used as an emergency helicopter pad. We played golf. Just the one hole. They used to have a three-hole golf course but it got washed away and I don't think anyone's got the heart for a rebuild. Interesting place to lose a golf ball. We couldn't all play so it seemed only sensible that John should caddie for me.

Sandi, David and Jim with their caddie at The Hyskeir International Open.

JOHN There was not much call for the use of drivers but Jim and Sandi managed to loft a couple of balls out over the rocks, diligently shouting 'Fore!'. There then followed a putting competition. Acting as caddie is not too arduous a task on this course. We enthusiastically hatched a plan to attract big-name sponsorship for the next Hyskeir International Open Tournament.

SANDI In four years' time there will be no more keepers growing Brobdingnagian veg. The new satellite navigational equipment and computers have made them redundant. I shan't feel as safe at sea as I do when I know that beneath the friendly flashing beacon there's a man checking the weather reports and stirring a delicious seagull curry.

SEAGULLS FOR DINNER

Henry VIII served roasted seagulls at his state banquets and parrot pie was popular on Captain Cook's *Endeavour*, although the captain wasn't the cook.

 JOHN The seclusion and tranquillity were attractive until set against David's recollections of a winter storm in the Shetlands when waves went right over the top of the 267-foot-high lighthouse. I shuddered and wanted to get on for Barra before the unsettled weather could take a turn for the worse.

Tom was getting anxious. We were about six or seven hours from Barra with no wind to speak of and ominous clouds on the horizon. As it turned out it was an uneventful motor-sail in steady rain. Everyone was in good spirits, comforted by the sight of Barra all the way from the lighthouse.

'We are so lucky,' Pol said wiping the steam from his glasses. 'There are people who spend every summer cruising the Western Isles and never make it to the Outer Hebrides.'

 SANDI We sailed into Castlebay, a beautiful little harbour dominated by the remains of the castle of the Clan MacNeil, standing isolated in the heart of the bay. Beyond the castle, the modern terminal for the Oban ferry showed an island determined not to be left in the past. The town of Castlebay is small and grey with a bank, a post office and a couple of general stores. There are 1500 people on Barra but it was past 10 at night when we arrived and we saw no one.

DAY 36 Barra

JOHN Barra is bleak. The rain is coming down in a steady drizzle, making the landscape stern and unwelcoming. The houses have a dismal uniformity. There are a few attractive stone cottages and larger houses but anything new is a charmless chalet bungalow. Mind you, if the weather is like this most of the time I suppose the exterior appearance of your home is not wildly important.

SANDI It is the most extraordinarily barren island. A Nordic assembly of rocky outcrops, peat bogs and small houses with bright, red-tiled roofs. It is only the dour grey Church of Scotland churches and graveyards which remind you of Britain. I found a graveyard where a chap called Robert Taylor was buried with his first wife, Mary Taylor, and his second wife, Mary Taylor. I wonder if he deliberately chose two women with the same name so as not to get confused. Either that or perhaps the person marking up the gravestone forgot that he'd already written Mary Taylor once and did it twice.

We've been away five weeks now. I stood in the graveyard trying to assemble any thoughts about where we had been. All I could think of was how far we still had to journey.

> Time goes, you say? Ah, no!
> Alas, Time stays, we go.
> AUSTIN DOBSON

DAY 37 Barra

JOHN We're still hoping the weather will improve to make a trip to St Kilda possible. To take our minds off the weather we went to see one of Barra's great claims to fame – the airport on the beach. The runway is only visible at low tide when the plane lands directly on the sand. The safety-crew checks the depth of any standing water before planes are allowed in. The mist was so low that we were taken by surprise when the small twin-propellered aircraft made a spectacular appearance out of the low rain-clouds, came in round the bay and landed on the wide sandy beach.

OVERLEAF: *More British summer weather on the way to Barra.*

POSTCARD
NUMBER 7:
*Four shades of
grey on Barra.*

POSTCARD NUMBER 8:
*Barra International
Airport, Club Lounge.*

 As the passengers disembarked we sat in the terminal building talking to Jane, who splits her day between being a flight controller, a ticket agent and sending in weather reports. She also made us tea. Jane said they get a few tourists coming in; the majority of passengers are locals or other people with business on the island. Many of the locals were visiting relatives in hospital in Glasgow. The Health Board pays for the patient's flight and there is a special, half-price, fare of eighty-two pounds for close relatives. On top of that they have to pay for food and accommodation, an additional hardship which adds considerably to their worry about the sick relative.

Jane loves living on Barra, even though it can be foul in winter. The only thing that gets her down is that, on an island of 1500 people, everyone knows everyone else's business. This has its benefits – as we saw on Eigg – but Jane said there are times when she would really like to go out for a meal without knowing the private lives of everyone in the restaurant and the kitchen, and all of them knowing hers.

SANDI Debate on the island rages about building a permanent tarmac runway. I don't think they should. You wouldn't get the seafood. The firemen came in from chasing the plane with a large bucket of cockles. It seems the dune-buggy churns up all the cockles on the beach as it passes. They simply scoop them up into a bucket, leave them in water for a bit and then microwave them in the terminal building. A hot cockle straight off the runway. Delicious. I wanted to phone Rick Stein but Jeremy, our over-enthusiastic producer, has a thing about the Met Office in Southampton so we called them instead.

Nice chaps and lasses. The man told me that there would be a twenty-four-hour window with the winds going southerly. He said this would be our only foreseeable opportunity to get as far west as St Kilda and the island of Hirta, our boat's namesake. Everyone got very excited and rushed off in search of Tom.

JOHN Our enthusiasm was abruptly deflated when we told the 'good news' to Tom. He angrily demanded to know what someone sitting in an office in Southampton knew about conditions in the Outer Hebrides and beyond. When he had calmed down he explained that twenty-four hours might be enough to do the round trip but, thanks to the recent weather conditions, we would need longer to let the massive Atlantic swell settle down before we set off. If possible we will head north to the Isle of Harris and Lewis tomorrow and make a final decision there about St Kilda. I am not sure if it was the miserable weather, our extreme tiredness, Tom's crushing temper or a mix of all these things, but Sandi and I sat down and tried to recall when Jane had said the next flight out would be.

SANDI When in doubt in the UK, visit a historic monument. There are enough of them. Kiessimul Castle in the harbour is not open every day and you need to grab your chance. From the edge of the bay it appears to be the encapsulation of romance, rising up out of the waters like some monolithic call to honour, love and arms.

JOHN After 800 years as the clan seat, Kiessimul fell into disrepair in the 1830s. A century later, the forty-fifth chief, Robert MacNeil, an American, decided to restore the castle to its former glory. From a distance it still looks magnificent set on its rock in the middle of the bay, but inside it is taken over with partitioning and ugly modern windows that would be more at home in a second-rate B & B than a romantic fortress. It's a strange and dreary place, not helped by the fact that it was absolutely chucking it down and we were soaked to the skin.

THE MACNEILS OF KIESSIMUL

The original castle was built to protect the MacNeil clan. Entirely surrounded by the sea, the castle boasts a freshwater spring inside which, as well as being able to fish from the ramparts, meant the family could resist a siege for a very long time. They were a tough bunch, the MacNeils – the 'Terror of the Western Isles'. There's a story that the chief of the clan, MacNeil, used to employ a bard who, when the Chief had eaten, would go up into the hills and shout 'The MacNeil has supped. Now the princes of the world may eat'. No inferiority complexes there.

 The castle does have one bit of historical merit – it contains the three oldest privies in the whole of the UK. The oldest one, at the bottom of the dungeon, is washed out by the tide. It's a flushing tidal toilet. I'm in favour of flushing toilets but they don't really make an afternoon pass.

Tom has decided that the window is suitable for us to move up to Tarbert tomorrow. It's an odd business, this. You never can be settled. You never know where you are. The winds change and you're off again. I must say I don't feel a bit like going.

MORE JOBS TO CONSIDER

1 Beach-runway fireman on Barra (similar to *Baywatch* in America – less glamorous but bigger cockles).
2 After-supper bard to the Chief of the MacNeils.

DAY 38 Barra to Harris

SHIP'S LOG: WINDS WESTERLY FORCE 5,
SEA STATE MODERATE, SHOWERS.

Off again, the usual early start. I'm sorry that we never saw Barra other than in the rain and fog but I liked her. The others felt no attraction for the place and were quite happy to depart.

We actually sailed straight off the mooring. No engine at all. What a thrill. Sandi Staysail and Johnny Jib did our now popular double-act on the foresails. The sun came out for the first time in half a lifetime. Sailing can be a heck of a lot more fun if things aren't pouring down on you and you have a really great view of the Outer Hebridean islands – Eriskay, plus South and North Uist and, between them, Benbecula.

JOHN I have revised my opinion this morning: the sun shone and Barra was a different place. The white sands and clear blue waters looked positively Caribbean. The westerly wind, although carrying cool air from the Arctic, gave us a perfect breeze which *Hirta* relished as she rolled comfortably through the light swell. My faith in our adventure was restored: I was at one with my fellows, our

Sandi Staysail and Johnny Jib.

ship and the sea. I could have been in any time and as the traditional music of the Chieftains drifted up from the saloon I half-closed my eyes to imagine a sea full of the galleons and schooners of boyhood fantasy.

WHISKY GALORE

In the early part of this century, a large steamship, the *Politician*, foundered off the small island of Eriskay. The villagers were able to salvage most of the cargo, which included 265 000 bottles of whisky. The writer, Compton Mackenzie, lived on Barra and wrote the event into a story called *Whisky Galore*, later one of the great Ealing comedies.

We were heading north for the Isle of Harris, which isn't a separate island at all but a small bit that sticks out from the Isle of Lewis. Pol says the islands are heavily categorized as either Catholic or Protestant. If you go to the Catholic islands you have a jolly good time but the Protestants are rather dour and on a Sunday nothing happens at all. Odd that they can be so close together and yet have such different ways of life. Many of the houses we spotted stood entirely isolated. The *Neighbours* theme tune kept running through my head. You could set a really dull soap opera up here where characters don't meet for weeks.

It's a curious thought that a crofter living in a small stone house on, say, the tip of Barra, with the winds constantly buffeting them as they look out to sea, is part of the same country as a shop assistant in a bedsit overlooking Piccadilly Circus. The contrast of lifestyles in the UK is far greater than I could have imagined.

Tom poured over the charts as we headed for East Loch Tarbert. Panic soon bubbled up. Tom decided Tarbert was too small and it was all very dangerous, etc., etc. As we made it into the port, we looked behind us to see the biggest, most gleaming white yacht I've ever seen in my life steaming in, happily unperturbed. A huge thing with ranged portholes, a glazed wheelhouse and uniformed crew busy beneath vast radar domes. A Gulliver to our lilliputian skiff. A chap stood on deck calling 'Hello, Tom' with a loudhailer while six gents in full tuxedos stood about clutching cocktails. Pol said the boat would have left little change from ten million pounds. They eyed Tarbert and us from above, waved and casually turned to sail on.

Tarbert is a small town without much to commend it. The quayside where the ferry runs was deserted. Probably because it was a Sunday and I think they're Protestant. Half a mile up the road we stopped at The Harris Hotel. If you miss 1950s holidays, this is the hotel for you.

Dinner is served when the 7.30 p.m. gong sounds. By 7.32, the old dining room doors swing shut, their brass handles and large engraved glass panels of ornamental peacocks daring latecomers to enter. A waitress in a white pinny stands beside the closed hatch through to the kitchen as she oversees the beige dining room. The embossed wallpaper creeps like mould up the walls. The guests sip their orange juice starters, careful not to spill a drop on the starched cloths and mindful of the unwritten rule against conversation. A bottle of white wine stands warming by the fire. The hatch snatches open and shut to expel a plate of despondent vegetables. Travelling at the pace we are, we are all tired and hungry. It is nice to have a really good solid meal. Unfortunately, that is not available on the Isle of Harris.

LAZY BEDS

The fishermen of Harris also grow crops and they do it in the most infertile of places. On strips of barren rock, they lay out lazy beds, growing areas made up of layers of seaweed and other organic stuff to create a bed for vegetables. They are said to be some of the finest vegetables in the country. They do not appear on the Harris Hotel menu.

DAY 39 Tarbert

Tom has decided that with the winds going to northerly by the end of the week we are in danger of becoming stuck here. He has moved *Hirta* round to the smaller island of Scalpay. There is a window for us to set off in the morning. The only possible sensible destination is Orkney. It is a thirty-hour passage to Stromness. There is absolutely no hope of visiting St Kilda.

DAY 40 Scalpay to Cape Wrath

SHIP'S LOG: WINDS LIGHT VARIABLE, BECOMING STRONGER
LATER, SEA STATE MODERATE.

We left Harris at 8 a.m., uncertain of our destination. With the weather patterns so confused that even the forecasters seem to be guessing, Tom feels it best to get across the Minch, the large body of water which separates the Isle

of Lewis from the mainland, while the going is reasonably good. If these conditions hold we can carry on all the way to Orkney; if they deteriorate we could seek shelter sooner. Ideally, Tom would have found us a safe haven and waited for steadier conditions, so he was understandably irked by the pressure to keep going, but if we delay now we might lose a week.

 We might be heading for either Kinlochbervie or Loch Nedd on the mainland, but nobody seems to know. I am befuddled by never, ever, knowing where we're going. Never being in charge of my own direction. Constantly at the mercy of the winds and other people's whims. We ploughed out to sea and grades of grey not knowing where we were going or when we would get there. I wonder if we have spent long enough anywhere to really get to know the place. No doubt we know more about each other than about Britain. We drank a lot of tea.

MILK AT SEA

There is no fridge or even cool-box so fresh milk is at a premium. James Gordon Bennet Jr, an American, was so keen on fresh dairy products at sea that he had a special padded room built for a cow on board his steam yacht *The Lysistrata*. We've barely got room for a tin of Marvel.

We saw a number of fishing boats earlier in the day; now we are quite alone. The coastline is beautiful, rugged and deserted: shafts of sunshine bring out the most dramatic shades of greens on the hills and the cliffs change from black to light brown. The sky is extraordinary: above us bright blue while all around clouds mass in all shapes and sizes; some black, some white, and every shade of grey in between. I thought I had learnt all there was to know about the colour grey in those dingy Lebanese cells. There, it had been only depressing yet now, with the vast range of tones, it was uplifting. Large choppy seas still approach us from all directions so that *Hirta* dips, rears up and swoops down again without any rhythm. The decision has been taken to sail on to Orkney.

There's an air of tension and excitement on board: tension at the thought of a night passage through these dangerous waters in uncertain conditions, and excitement that, past Cape Wrath, we will turn eastwards after following the compass north for five weeks. The prospect of reaching Orkney, the half-way point on our circumnavigation of Britain, has us predicting 'It's all downhill from here'.

Today is also the longest day of the year, so we're to witness the Summer Solstice at sea.

Earlier, as I prepared a hot supper for the night sail, I played a Van Morrison tape at full volume, so as to hear it above the engine noise, and as the rice boiled and the meat and vegetables simmered, I leapt around madly on the bucking dance-floor, as if by stamping and bouncing around I would train my body to be able to move freely in these unstable conditions. I had just listened to the song 'Wonderful Remark' and its line 'clinging to some other rainbow' when I took the food up on deck and saw a bay and cliffs haloed by a vivid rainbow. I felt certain no harm would come to us.

About 9 o'clock in the evening on the night of the Summer Solstice, we rounded Cape Wrath, the sharp top-left-hand corner of Britain. It is also home to some of the most notorious waters in the British Isles, although the name is less fearful than it would first seem. It comes from the old Norse word *Hvraf*, meaning turning point. Here, the Vikings would have turned down the Minch and along past the Highlands of Scotland.

We had travelled the whole of the west coast of Britain. The sun shone down on the cliffs and above it a full, translucent moon, pulling and pushing at our waters, stood proud. The light is so intense here in the northern part of Scotland that it is as if your eyes have suddenly focused for the very first time. I mourned my inability to capture colour.

Feeling as though we ought to celebrate, I pulled a bottle of Trawlers rum up on to the deck. I felt overwhelmed by the achievement. It was the first time even Tom had made this passage and I asked him if the responsibilities that he faces in such difficult waters spoil the pleasure of the moment. He turned on me in unexpected and inexplicable rage.

'There is no pleasure,' he bellowed. 'No pleasure at all. Only in arriving.'

Everyone was silenced. We turned to watch the moon rise above the cliffs but there was no pleasure in it.

I was shocked by the content and venom of Tom's response; I could see no point in putting yourself through such agonies if the only enjoyment was in the destination. I suppose Tom, unlike us, knows what it can be like; but why do it unless the experience is rewarding?

At any rate, with our turn eastwards the choppiness disappeared and the ride became more comfortable. It was still very light: Cape Wrath lighthouse stood out brightly with an almost full moon shining vividly above it in a deep blue sky. In the west the sun was still quite high, shining orange, white and pink through the higher strata of cloud. The low clouds were massive and could have been another mountainous coastline but for a little chink on the far horizon where a vivid orange flame of sunlight looked like a welcoming hearth on a bleak night.

DAY 41 Cape Wrath to Stromness

SANDI I couldn't sleep. I felt so distressed by our skipper's words and found I needed to sit on deck looking to the coast for comfort. Just after 1 a.m., Pol and I spotted the Strathy Point lighthouse. I knew it would be a long way off but it was comforting. It was an extremely cold and rather dull passage. From about 2.30 onwards we could see the Orkneys about 25 miles away. It never really got dark. The lights sort of faded down and then faded up again. I have grown accustomed to grey.

I spent some time thinking about emptying the rum bottle. Not to drink it. I wanted to chuck the bottle into the sea with a message calling for help. I couldn't see the harm. People have been doing it since ancient Greek times. Elizabeth I actually had an Official Uncorker of Ocean Bottles because the country got so many. The best message ever was uncorked by some chap who found a thirteen-year-old scrap of paper washed up in a bottle which said: 'To avoid all confusion, I leave my entire estate to the lucky person who finds this bottle and to my attorney, Barry Cohen, share and share alike'. It was signed Daisy Alexander, heir to the twelve-million-dollar Singer sewing machine fortune. I didn't send one in the end. I couldn't think what to write. Besides, Tom was sleeping over the bottle locker.

JOHN Coming back on watch with Tom at 3 o'clock there was a little rain and the breeze had picked up a bit so Pol and Sandi had raised the foresails. Tom fixed a large rope called a preventer to the boom to stop the mainsail gybing. During our watch the rain became heavier and heavier, the wind moved round to come more directly from the south and reached peaks of gale force; 'blowing a bandit', as Tom put it. We could see Orkney dead ahead but it became more blurred by the minute as visibility deteriorated. To the south-west we caught glimpses of the mainland coast through the rain clouds scudding along it.

I was very tired and *Hirta* demanded all my concentration as she bucked through the waves like a wild horse. For a moment she would snap the reins from my grasp

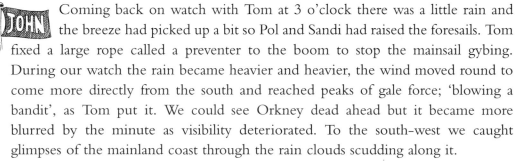

and veer off on her own path as I shouted in anger and frustration into the wind and driving rain. Gradually I would pull her back on course and for minutes we would charge on through the seas, my body tensely braced at odd angles to keep myself in the cockpit. The water around us rose and fell dramatically. I watched fulmars glide just above the surface and disappear as though landing, only to reappear seconds later from behind another mound of water. Through the squalls we could see the Old Man of Hoy, the stack of rock standing alone off Hoy, the first island in the Orkney group. As a boy I had seen a film of people climbing it. Looking at it now I thought they must be crazy.

Orkney's tides are notorious and as we went through the Sound of Hoy they doubled our own speed of over 7 knots. As we went further up the Sound and the channel grew narrower, the sensation of acceleration became almost surreal; it was as if we were stationary and the grazing cows in the meadows on the shores were being spun past us on a conveyor belt. I thought of Keenan's dream of a boat zooming along a coastline with a mind of its own. There was no one within hailing distance, however, so I could not enquire the way to Norway.

SANDI I was exhausted to the very heart of my being. The others lay bound in their bunks by their storm cloths as the wind heeled *Hirta* over and over and I attempted to lash myself into my cot. I fought for sleep for a while and then gave up. On deck, the rain had now set in with an incredible vengeance as we adopted absurd angles to stay with the boat. By 6 o'clock we were coming in at a breathtaking lick towards the outer holme, or harbour, of Stromness.

The rope preventer now stopped us from bringing the sails down as we entered the harbour at speed with no way of stopping. There was more shouting and swearing than I've ever heard in a single outburst. The rain fell in matching amounts of temper and I saw nothing of Stromness. We could have been arriving in Cairo for all I cared. We were being shouted at or trying to deal with the sails or suddenly dropping to our knees to give the skipper a clearer view. Once on my knees I found I was unable to get up off the deck.

JOHN I felt profoundly in tune with the boat and totally sure-footed as I leapt about the deck attending to the ropes. I was too confident to worry about Tom's abuse but too tired to appreciate Sandi's jokes. 'Stromness has the lowest average rainfall in the Orkneys; it is famous for its mild climate,' she bantered over the raging gale.

Tom brought us right on to our mooring buoy and Pol and I struggled to get a rope attached to it while the wind drove solid sheets of rain and hailstones at us.

My heels set up a violent protest about the hours of unnatural posture they had endured crossing this little corner of the Atlantic Ocean. Even in my state of exhaustion the pain seemed almost comical and did nothing to dent my elation at having taken part in a dramatic twenty-four-hour sea passage. This had been the passage which made it all worthwhile.

 I was so tired, so wet and so miserable that I really did not think I could continue with the second half of our journey.

Stromness

We slept most of yesterday afternoon and have explored today. Stromness is on Mainland, the largest island of the Orkneys. The sun has been out all day adding to the pleasure of walking from the harbour through the town's winding cobbled streets. The window displays look as if they have not changed since the 1950s and many have old fashioned sunscreens across them. I got the impression of a confident town.

We wandered past narrow passages with unlikely names like The Khyber Pass, glancing at ourselves in shop windows filled with northern arts and crafts. After six weeks at sea I don't think either one of us is a pretty sight. John looks like the front cover of a book entitled *Mr Rugged Gives up on Grooming* and I wouldn't look out of place crawling from beneath one of the local standing stones. We popped in to a hairdresser's.

It was the sort of hairdresser's I seem to remember from the 1960s. Large bell-like hairdriers pinned down lobster-faced women who had had things done very tightly to their hair. The owner emerged to fill reception. Kathleen is a coiffeur in the Amazonian tradition. No hair would dare to remain out of place under her cheerful but determined charge. She gave us a fine haircut each and then took us home to her dairy farm. I've never been home with a hairdresser before.

Our initial impression of Orkadians is one of contentment. A happy-go-lucky not very materialistic people but, as with all the small communities we have visited, there is another side. The local newspaper was full of detail about a murder

OPPOSITE: *Kirkwall, Orkney.*

investigation in Kirkwall. Two weeks previously, an Indian waiter had been murdered by two white men wearing balaclavas. Also on the front page, although the newspaper made no link between these stories, was coverage about an Asian woman taxi-driver who had been abused by two young white farmers. They had exposed themselves to her and threatened to get balaclavas and shoot her.

That evening we went out and by chance our taxi-driver was the woman I had read about. The local paper coverage hadn't been accurate. She wasn't Asian at all, but from Saudi Arabia. She'd been living in the Orkneys for nine years and spoke with passion about the streak of racism which she said permeated all the islands. She bitterly recounted that, while the young men were threatening to kill her, people on the quayside had been cheering, laughing and whistling and egging them on. This was a very different portrait of an island community. While the great urban centres of Britain have swelled as ethnic melting pots, the same does not seem to be true of the coastal and small island communities.

The unspoken racism issue remained in our minds as we ate our supper at the Empire Chinese restaurant. It was Chinese food all right, but we didn't see a single Chinese person. The place was staffed entirely by white Orkadians. It may not have meant anything, but it was curious. If you go to the Empire, don't have the soup.

'Too bad that all the people who know how to run the country are busy driving taxi-cabs and cutting hair.'

GEORGE BURNS

 Kirkwall

We woke to find the world shrunk by heavy fog. No hope of crossing the Pentland Firth today. Maybe tomorrow. Maybe not. At times the fog over the water seems like a light mist compared to the blackness in my mind. I do look forward to the journey but now it is often just to the journey's end, to home and a cessation of new impressions.

Kirkwall is the capital of Mainland. Another extremely pretty small town with narrow streets and shop displays of women's clothing frozen in the 1950s. I needed some time to myself and went for a walk.

St Magnus Cathedral, first thing in the morning, was full of Japanese tourists snapping away, and me. I wandered through the magnificent building reading the old plaques to people who've died over the years. I find I've become obsessed with counting how many perished at sea. A lot of them were sad; people in the seventeenth century with eight children of whom only one or two survived. I found I was reading the list of names with some anxiety to see who'd actually made it. I don't know how any parent could have withstood the pain of such loss.

My favourite tribute was to William Balchie Balfour. He was a missionary who had died in his thirties but not before he had translated the Bible into the Central African languages. No doubt exactly what the Central Africans needed. Think how grateful they must have been that he managed to 'turn the slave and the savage away from the heathen path'.

JOHN This afternoon we said goodbye to Pol and welcomed Tom's wife Ros and their daughter Hannah as our new shipmates. I am sad to see Pol go, he has been a good companion and a tolerant instructor. On the sail here to Orkney I felt a closer bond, of being a real team-mate, as we raced around the boat making her ready for our arrival in Stromness.

Ros and Hannah join us in Orkney.

SANDI It will be strange to set sail with new blood. Now we shall have to pull our weight. We were both anxious and excited. Hannah is fifteen and tall enough to play centre-forward for a US women's basketball team. With her mother she brings the total on board up to eight, but rather improves the female/male ratio.

The swelling in my hands has been diagnosed as a repetitive strain injury, aggravated by the heavy work on board. A physiotherapist has put both my wrists and my hands in splints. I do not know whether I shall be able to function as a crew member. John says he always knew I'd lose my grip.

DAY 44 Stromness

SHIP'S LOG: LIGHT VARIABLE WINDS,
SEA STATE CALM.

JOHN We set off in sunshine past the island of Cava with the gas flame of the Flotta oil terminal burning clearly behind it. As we entered the channel between Hoy and another island, Fara, Tom and Ros warned that a fog bank was forming up ahead. It looked to me to be little more than light haze but they were right; within moments we were utterly engulfed in fog, a complete whiteout. Tom sent me below to keep an eye on the echo-sounder while he probed the fog a little to see if there was a break in it. I came back up on deck some time later when he had given me the all-clear and had to look twice at the compass to convince myself that we were now going in the opposite direction. Tom was not going to take us further into the fog in these unpredictable waters and we were returning to Stromness. I was relieved: I could see nothing in any direction and the air had a chill, damp edge to it which seemed to creep, full of menace, deep into your bones. If I buy a boat it will have a radar.

SANDI Unexpectedly back in the same place. I took John souvenir-shopping. It's tricky to know what to buy to remind you of a particular place. We agreed on an island. Well, we'd seen so many we felt it was time we owned one. Fortunately there was one for sale. Only eighty thousand pounds. We popped in to the estate agent's for the particulars.

It is the Holm of Grimbister, or 'our island' as we began to think of it. Forty acres in the Bay of Firth, complete with house and running water. Annoyingly, John and I were not the only interested party. A family from Glossop in Derbyshire

OPPOSITE: *Sandi wearing her attractive new hand splints.*

were looking around as we arrived. John and I tried to appear casual. We didn't want to up the price. The husband said he was a paint technician (John explained that that's re-spraying cars and panel-beating). The man had only ever been a paint technician. I eyed him. He didn't look as though he would know one end of a sheep from the other and he admitted that he knew nothing about farming. Maybe everyone dreams of owning a self-sufficient island.

The low tide had revealed a rocky causeway. A familiar fog had settled in with such a vengeance that although the island is cheek by jowl with Mainland, it was actually impossible to see it. Nor could you see from one end to the other of the 200-foot-long causeway. I stuck close to John. I didn't want to find myself marooned with a paint technician and his Glossop family. We slipped over seaweed and carried the strong smell of fish on our boots on to the long grass of the Holm of Grimbister. Three or four seals poked their heads up in the bay and laughed.

A remarkably young estate agent, with red hair matched by a carroty-coloured face, began his pitch. He seemed to think that it was a feature to point out that there are no trees on the island. Too much wind, you see, for a tree to be able to stand. To be honest it put me off buying the place. I can't imagine I'd be too steady anywhere the wind's strong enough to knock trees down. I didn't say anything. The young man liked his job. He confided: 'There aren't many jobs on the island where you get to wear a suit'. Knee-high in soggy long grass, I couldn't see the thrill of his charcoal grey three-piece, but he was happy. Like every estate agent I've ever met, he claimed that the house at the centre of the island was entirely habitable.

Through a small out-house entrance we walked into the principal room of the tiny croft. There is electricity on the island, but by the time it's travelled out there, the power is so exhausted that the bulbs burn with no confidence. This was not a place where you'd want to try to use a hairdrier in a hurry. I was soaked. A hairdrier seemed like a really good idea. Mr Suit announced that this large bare room, perhaps 7 feet wide by about 10 feet long, was the kitchen-cum-dining room-cum-living room-cum-bedroom. This was confirmed by the large double bed wedged in next to the Aga and small fridge. Mrs Paint Technician gave a sharp intake of breath, her eyes suddenly revealing the true beauty of Glossop. Her husband did what men do when viewing houses. He banged confidently on the wall, saying: 'Yes, I could do a lot with this'. Perhaps he could, he's used to panel-beating.

The out-buildings were crammed with mouldering paraphernalia and wonderful wooden milling equipment. Great high boxes just waiting to be filled with barley or wheat to tumble down oak shoots into wide hooped wooden barrels. Out in the testimony-to-weeds garden, our man from Glossop was increasingly determined that this was A Good Idea. His florid-faced wife grew more and more despondent as he announced with confidence that he could easily raise the money. 'I've got a very nice house. It's an end house with a driveway.' John and I backed off and left them to it. We went to buy a plastic sewing kit with a picture of the cathedral on it as a souvenir instead.

What is it about Britain today that so many people dream of the rural idyll? Of 'getting away from it all' and back to the soil? Of re-creating Ma and Pa Larkin's countryside existence? It is a strange dream because the people who know the truth about rural life, the farmers, generally seem desperate to get out and swap it for a different way of life.

DAY 45 — Stromness to Wick

JOHN We were up at 3 this morning but the fog was still so bad we had a cup of tea on deck and turned in again. I tossed and turned, remembering the disorientation in that eerie, cold fog. It had spooked me; the glories of the sail here were overshadowed by nervous anticipation of what we might encounter in the Pentland Firth. We are due back in Falmouth in five weeks; the obligation to keep constantly on the move becomes very dispiriting at times.

SANDI When I re-awoke, the morning was mine to kick around Kirkwall. I walked back up to my friend the cathedral. My plan was foiled by the arrival of the King and Queen of Norway, which is not what you'd expect. A microcosm of a welcoming crowd waited behind unnecessary metal barriers. Four women holding a Greenpeace placard represented the only dissent from the gathering of Orkadians waving Norwegian flags. I wonder if they keep the flags just in case royalty turn up or whether they're something people have in their homes anyway? Some boys stood around wearing the top half of Boy Scout uniforms over kilts while two policemen in white gloves and one motor cycle cop tried to look important. It was a kind of miniature royal visit.

The King stepped out of a Rolls-Royce. It's always slightly disappointing when you see a king and he isn't wearing a crown but a blue mac. He waved politely to me, I like to think, as the Queen stepped out, a rather beautiful woman in a bright cerise shawl. I felt a bit sorry for them as they moved up the steps to meet what looked like a lot of dull dignitaries.

JOHN The tide was in our favour again at 4 o'clock in the afternoon. I had phoned home.

'Lovely weather!' said my brother. 'It's so hot you can hardly sit outside.'

'Great,' I said, wiping the mist from the phone booth window.

With the visibility still so hazy I wasn't optimistic, but Tom had programmed various points along the passage into the GPS, the satellite navigation device. This small box has been dubbed 'Henry the Navigator' and is Tom's one concession towards high-technology. He felt confident that Henry would see us through and that only the densest fog would send us back to Stromness again.

SCAPA FLOW

Europe's best dive. It was here, after the First World War, that some seventy ships of the surrendered German fleet were brought under guard. At a signal they all scuppered themselves and went down. The bottom of Scapa Flow is absolutely littered with all sorts of horrid naval wreckage.

SANDI The winds were a peaceful force 3 as *Hirta*'s engine put the Orkneys behind us. I looked back, still amazed that these treeless and barren islands are part of the British Isles. They really are so very un-British to look at. They would not look out of place in my native Scandinavia.

Into the notorious waters of the Pentland Firth. Tides of up to 7 knots can race in these waters and there are stories of destroyers going at full speed but making no headway against the opposing waters. We were lucky and things were relatively calm. We took a bearing for Duncansby Head, the most north-easterly corner of Britain. There's a lighthouse there which stands some 300 feet above the sea. The Firth has been known to throw rocks up with the waves and smash them against windows at the top of the beacon. We were quite happy not to bear witness to such fury and even more delighted not to work for the local window replacement company.

JOHN As we motor-sailed past Duncansby Head, Tom came up from checking the charts with a big grin on his face.

'I am going to give you a new course,' he said to Sandi at the helm, 'which I think you will approve. Your heading is 180 degrees – south!' I had never heard Sandi say 'Aye, aye, skipper,' with such heartfelt enthusiasm.

OPPOSITE: *Unbelievably, Sandi and John are left in charge leaving Orkney.*

146

Five hours later at Wick I jumped, or rather rolled, on to a fishing boat with our mooring ropes and made fast. It may have been clumsy but I was relieved to have done this successfully as it had formerly been one of Pol's duties. Despite our best efforts we are still unsure of ourselves and need to be reminded that Pol has been sailing all his life, as have the Cunliffes – Hannah had been back and forth across the Atlantic before she was five.

JOHN O'GROATS

Bit of a publicity job, old John O'Groats. It is alleged to be the most northerly point of mainland Britain. It was named after a Dutchman, John de Groats, who started one of the first ferry services out towards the Orkneys. It was a selling point that you came up to John O'Groats and then from there you could leap further north to the Orkneys by ferry. In fact the furthest point north is Dunnet Head, which was obscured from our view by relentless fog.

POSTCARD NUMBER 9: *Not the most northern point of Britain.*

At one time there were over 1000 boats in the fishing fleet in Wick but those days have passed. Much of the town now relies on the Caithness glassworks for employment. From the docks, the town stepped back in grey ranks of hewn Scottish stone. We walked up to McKay's Hotel for a drink and a shower. A faded legend on the side of the building proclaimed it The Temperance Hotel, but not while we were in town.

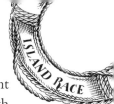

John says the sound of the Velcro strips that fasten my splints, and both the front and sleeves of our sailing jackets, remind him of the tape they used to bind him with in Beirut. He didn't say it as anything except fact but now everyone has become incredibly cautious about openings and closings when he is around.

DAY 46 Wick

One month exactly until we must complete our journey and we're fog-bound again. I'm delighted to find that I have been at the forefront of the news. A large article in *The Press and Journal* (Caithness and Sutherland edition) about the Norwegian King and Queen's visit to Orkney is accompanied by a photo in which you can almost see me waving in the background. The actual story, however, is one of tragedy. A prize-winning Aberdeen Angus bull, called Heathland's Buzzmarti (known as Buzzi for short), had been specially shampooed in readiness for a royal visit to Quanterness Farm in St Ola, but because the state visit was delayed by eighty minutes due to fog, the farm had to be dropped from the royal schedule. "'Buzzi was looking marvellous and very proud of himself this morning,'" said Christine Harkess, whose husband Scott runs the 1000-acre farm. [I bet Christine just sits around all day and lets Scott get on with it.] "The cows thought he was a new bull. He and we are very disappointed not to have met the King.'"

The article also mentions that the crowd of 350 people included a small group of Greenpeace protesters. Well … I saw four women and a placard of a whale. But I like the idea of it being a small group. The journalist went on to say that the royal flight was delayed while Kirkwall airport was closed by a thick 'haar'. This is a brand-new word for me which I intend to employ the minute we set sail again.

Further news — an elderly holiday-maker was found dead after paddling on a Harris beach yesterday. Well, I'm not surprised. It's bloody freezing.

Wick reminds me a lot of Edinburgh with its over-sized grey granite buildings. Things are obviously not entirely tickety-boo in Wick. The estate agent's was packed with potential property including the large central town church. I overhead a man talking to a friend in the street: 'I just can't stand having nothing to do for any longer.' Today, the news is that the Rosyth naval base and dockyard looks likely to be axed. The Scottish *Sun* newspaper carries the headline 'Drop Dead Scotland'. Depression hangs in the air like forgotten Christmas decorations in June.

Wick to Peterhead

SHIP'S LOG: FOG CLEARING,
WINDS NORTH-EASTERLY FORCE 3.

SANDI South, south, past the Moray Firth and on to Peterhead. Rather a nice fresh wind as we approached the low skyline on another pigeon-coloured day. Every city looks so different from the sea than it does from the centre of the town. From a fair distance, we could see the small lighthouse and breakwaters which mark Peterhead Harbour. It took us a long time to arrive but for once everyone ignored our impossible schedule and relaxed into the sailing. When the pressure is off, it really is fun.

As we grow accustomed to the vagaries of wind and tide and a slower, much slower pace of life, I have been thinking about speed. *Hirta* was a fast boat in her day but now she can make all of us champ at the bit. You can make dinner in a microwave in minutes, fly at supersonic speeds, get photos developed in an hour and so on, but what are we all doing with the precious time we've saved? Watching *Blind Date*.

Peterhead is quite a small, quiet affair with run-of-the-mill shops. The locals seemed more likely than most to shout at their children in the street and clip them round the ear but perhaps we'd hit a bad day. We scouted out some serious food and found quite a choice. There was the National Mission to Deep-sea Fishermen who were offering a special on egg and chips. We settled on a small café, where a ham salad consisted of two pieces of see-through ham and alleged new potatoes which had not been new for a generation. John sighed as we reached for the salad cream to disguise yet another British failure at the simple meal. I don't think eating out is a big thing in Peterhead.

COMPASS CURIOSITY

You can use your watch as a compass. If you hold it horizontally at noon with the hands pointing at the sun then they will be facing due south. Six o'clock will be north, 9 o'clock will be west and 3 o'clock east. If it is before or after noon, point the hour-hand at the sun. South will be midway between the hour-hand and 12. At 10 in the morning, south will be at 11.

N.B. This is less successful with a digital watch.

OPPOSITE: *One man and his dog (Peterhead).*

Peterhead

Peterhead is nicknamed 'Blue Toon': one explanation is that it is so cold in winter the population turns blue; another story tells of the looting of a wreck full of bundles of blue cloth and an ensuing blue period in fashions.

 Markets, like tides, happen at unearthly hours. The Peterhead Fish Market, alleged to be the largest in Europe, was already in full swing when we arrived at 6.30 a.m. Raymond Fraser, the auctioneer for one of the fishing co-operatives, told me that, as it was a Saturday, the market was very quiet. It seemed anything but quiet to me and the speed of the auction was totally bewildering as skippers, auctioneers and buyers, stamping across the 2000 boxes of fish, moved swiftly down the hall.

'On weekdays there can be up to 9000 boxes of fish in the market and the prices are higher,' Raymond explained. 'But devout skippers won't sail on the Sabbath and so, to get a full week's fishing, they leave after midnight on Sunday and return for the Saturday market. They know they'll get a lower price for their catch but their faith's more important than their profit they say.'

Once the activity had died down we went into the market café for breakfast. It took supreme self-control to make headway with my bacon roll against the all-pervading stench of fish. Immune, Raymond told me about the local industry. It seems that the Peterhead fishermen are doing well, making plenty of money for their hard work – I am sure they deserve it for their week-long trips to sea in all conditions.

Although Peterhead's success marks a strong contrast with what we have heard about fishing in other ports, Raymond was not sanguine about the future. 'Fish consumption in Britain is dropping steadily and much of the catch here is exported to Europe where the competition grows ever stronger. Commissioning new boats is becoming rare, with rising costs and no government support.' He blamed this on the fishing community's feeble lobbying skills.

'Fishermen are a fiercely independent breed,' he said. 'Even within our co-operative, skippers won't give away their location over the radio or mobile phone as everyone has scanners and might go along to share a good catch. Messages home go by fax.'

We went back into the near-deserted sheds after breakfast and I asked Raymond, still looking very neat in his white coat, why he had come ashore. He looked at me aghast. 'I've never been a fisherman: one short trip in a trawler convinced me it was far too dangerous.'

An old man sprayed blue ink over the stock which failed to make the European minimum price and consigned it to the fishmeal factory. A pathetic end for the fish and all that effort.

FISH FACTS

1 An old Scottish law used to require fishermen to wear one gold earring. It was used to pay for their funeral expenses if they drowned and were washed ashore.

2 There was a taboo amongst ancient Egyptians against eating bream, pike or lepidotus. These three fish were supposed to have eaten the penis of the god Osiris when he was thrown into the Nile. Who thinks up these things?

3 A deep-sea fisherman told us what the men do with skate during long hours of boredom. It would be impolite to repeat it but suffice to say we won't ever eat it again. Skate have the same genitals as humans. Apparently, it's an offence for fishmongers to display them with their genitals showing. The skates', not the fishmongers'. Well, both, actually.

4 The freshest fish in the world was available at the Cistercian monastery in Alcobaca, Portugal. They built their kitchens with the Alcoa river flowing through them so they could catch fresh fish daily. Rick Stein! Wouldn't you be happy?

5 Scampi update: the angler fish is an incredibly wide-mouthed creature with a large sort of antenna which hangs like a lure over the top. Fishmongers cut the tails into strips and the fish then automatically curls up to resemble a prawn. It can be used for scampi. So can squat lobsters. How does anyone know what they're getting when they order scampi?

I sat outside the Dolphin Market Café, with George Foreman. We sipped dawn coffee as gargantuan gulls hung around waiting to scavenge. A gull the size of a pit bull terrier eyed my bacon sandwich. I handed it over without uttering a word.

George is a retired fisherman whose father and grandfather on both sides, and possibly his great-grandfather too, had all been fishermen. Now George's sons have taken up the mantle. George was incensed about the state of the fishing industry.

TOP: *The result of nodding once too often at the fish auction.*

LEFT: *Exchanging fish facts with Peterhead fisherman George Foreman.*

ABOVE: *Gulliver's travels, Peterhead-style.*

LEFT: *An unexpected visit from a village people person.*

He was confident that the volumes of rules coming out of Brussels are decimating his industry. We went down to the family boat. The strong smell of fish made my nostrils flare in a fine impression of the gills of a frightened cod. In his day, George worked steam-driven vessels and hauled the heavy nets in by hand.

The Venture, a vessel which cost two million pounds to build, was more akin to the bridge of the Starship Enterprise than anything I'd seen before. It was packed with technological equipment: radar, to show the size of the potential catch and the lay of the nets on the ocean floor; interior cameras for spying on the engine room and the net positions as automatic equipment shot them out to sea; a navigational computer; faxes; mobile phones and so on. George ran his hand over the million-pound controls. He was not without regrets.

'The fisherman,' he said, 'used to be a hunter but now he's the hunted – tracked down by an army of people with rules and regulations. There was a time when a fisherman could go to sea without so much as a pencil in his pocket but now it's nothing but form-filling and regulations.'

'There must be some positive things to all the modern developments,' I said. 'Does the new technology mean women can go to sea? I mean, you don't have to be strong any more.' George laughed and laughed and never answered.

The fog still lingered in the harbour. It trailed a soft wrap around the proud line of powerful fishing boats. I wandered along the docks to visit one of the oil-rig supply boats which ply their trade out of Peterhead. The great wide empty decks were buzzing with cables and ropes of unimaginable lengths. High above, the master of the ship, his hair moulded into unmanoeuvrable place, stood sentry.

'What sort of supplies do you take out?' I enquired.

He sniffed under his trim moustache. 'Oh, people all think that we take out, you know, bread and milk to the oil rig, but in fact it's a highly complicated list.' We went through the list. It was complicated.

'Who does take the bread and milk out, then?' I persisted.

He looked at his feet. 'Uh … we do.'

DAY 49 — Peterhead to Aberdeen

SHIP'S LOG: LIGHT WINDS,
SEA STATE CALM.

 We set sail at lunchtime for Aberdeen and once again the fog, the fog, the endless fog rolled in. We could hear the foghorns on our starboard side as we left Peterhead and sailed along past Buchan Ness. Everyone was sharp-eyed, watching the mists from the deck. At times like this there are no divisions between novices and old hands. We are united in the out-of-focus weather.

JOHN Once clear of Peterhead, Ros and I scrubbed down *Hirta*'s decks which had become covered in a film of fish scales, and cleaned her mooring ropes, filthy with oil and scum from her time in the working harbour. I was casually dropping a bucket over the side to let it half-fill when I found myself running aft, desperately hanging on to its rope. Visions of sea monsters dragging me down to the depths filled my mind as I knelt over the stern and wrestled the now disfigured bucket back aboard. I breathed a huge sigh of relief and looked round sheepishly, only to find Ros and Hannah recovering from the same experience. There was no monster other than the sea itself.

SANDI Ros made fresh pizza for lunch. There's no question that culinary matters have improved since her arrival. Indeed, the entire atmosphere seems more level and less unpredictable. John and I chatted, slept and took our turns as crew on the 25-mile trip south to Aberdeen. We feel so much more comfortable on the boat now and it is better for everyone.

OTHER JOBS
NO ONE MENTIONED AT SCHOOL

1 Fish auctioneer.
2 Harbour master.
3 Fishing net mender.

JOHN Arriving by sea anywhere is exciting; the anticipation builds from the first sighting through the binoculars to the gradual revelation of distinct buildings. I always wonder what other boats will be there, what the berth will be like and who we will meet. Aberdeen was on a different scale from anywhere else we have visited. The city itself has a classic Scots skyline with great grey spires towering over solid Victorian buildings. The harbour clearly proclaims its place at the heart of the oil industry; full of enormous ships, most of them supply vessels, with high bridges and decks the size of football fields where the great rig-mooring chains are transported. I did not get a proper sense of their size until I saw a man suspended in a cradle, half-way down a ship's side, painting: he looked no bigger than a fly.

SANDI The mainsail had to come down fairly sharpish and John and I enjoyed the silent co-operation of working as a team. We moved to get the head ropes ready without question and turned to get on with other jobs in hand. Well into the harbour system, we moored by a high quayside beyond the harbour office. An all-wood boat from Sweden came alongside for the night.

It had been a good sail, it was a fascinating harbour and new people came and went in instant friendships. I wished these feelings had happened earlier.

OPPOSITE: *Deckhand.*

DAY 50 Aberdeen to Arbroath

SHIP'S LOG: WINDS NORTH-EASTERLY FORCE 4,
SEA STATE MODERATE.

SANDI Sorry to give Aberdeen short shrift, but ever under pressure, we faced south on a sunny day. Everyone was in shirt-sleeves, cheerful, looking pale and shrivelled as oilskins and sweaters formed a growing mountain on the quarterberth. Ros tries to keep order but the three or four pegs available for the eight of us makes this an unequal task. Soon we were out of sight of land with the North Sea all around us. A minke whale splashed purposefully about behind us as a pod of seals and schools of dolphins cavorted in the waters of the North Sea.

JOHN I day-dreamed on deck as we cruised along. How relaxing it was to have so much time for reflection. It was absurd. We were delighted to be making about 5 miles an hour, ludicrously slow by motorway standards.

Ros sat with me on deck. 'Being on the sea when it's lovely is like a drug,' she said, sunning herself, 'you always want more. When it's like this I don't even mind polishing the woodwork or the lamps in the saloon.'

'What about bad weather?' I asked.

She lowered her voice and grinned. 'Then you're just glad to get there.'

CULINARY NOTE
Pork pies actually taste nice at sea.

DAY 51 Arbroath

JOHN We spent a wet day at the Arbroath Highland Games. All around, behind beer tents and fairground stalls, in the car park and on the sea wall, lone pipers practised for the day's competitions, filling the damp air with myriad laments, squeaks and marches.

SANDI A platform had been erected in one corner of the field. Beside it, anxious parents had settled with folding chairs and soggy picnics as they fussed over small children. Tartans of every hue and design swayed on the kilted kiddies. Some were rather jollier than others. Perhaps it was the luck of kinship which produced

160

a brilliant blue costume rather than a sombre brown. Several rather sheepish boys hung about dwarfed by tam-o'-shanters designed for larger heads. Rain dripped off the wide chapeaux as they stood like a row of expectant mushrooms.

To the connoisseur, the highland dance is no doubt a complex thing of beauty. To me it seemed mainly to consist of jigging from one foot to the other, bowing and putting your galoshes back on. I haven't seen so many galoshes since my childhood in the United States. The children tugged their rubber overshoes on to their dancing pumps and sploshed through the field for a reviving warm Ribena.

JOHN One boy, who can have been no more than seven years old, stamped his feet and shook his little fists as he went through an Irish jig with such gusto that I felt exhausted just watching. This is only half-way through the season – the dancers attend competitions every weekend from May to September. Such devotion smacked of fanaticism to me.

SANDI In the centre, the heavyweight competition – the bit of the games which even Americans will tell you about – was hotting up. Three exceptionally large gentlemen, all out of proportion as human beings and wearing runway-length kilts, grunted shot-puts up and away and dismissed heavy hammers with disdain. I picked up the 16-pound practice hammer, put it over my head and immediately dropped it behind me. I don't think it was going to be my event. The men moved on to the caber, tossing 120 pounds worth of pine trunk into the air.

Champion caber tosser.

ABOVE: *Number 143, Arbroath Games.*
OPPOSITE: *Yet another jolly piping tune.*

The question 'why?' hovered in the air. The boys had large feet so naturally I asked one of them what he was wearing under his kilt. Turned out to be boxer shorts, which I call a bit of a disappointment.

Over to one side, two judges sat listening to the piping competition. On a small square platform, lone pipers stood and mournfully dirged their way through what was alleged to be a jig, but seemed to be playing at the wrong speed. I asked the dashing young judge: 'Doesn't it all sound the same?'

He shook his head. 'Oh, no, no, no, you're not really listening properly.' I listened again. It all sounded the same. I am a piping philistine.

Tosser.

They're an independent lot in Arbroath. In 1320 Robert the Bruce gathered the Scottish nobles to sign the Declaration of Arbroath, asserting Scotland's independence from England. Today, in keeping with that heritage, the local Head Clansman, Chief Alistair Forsyth of that Ilk, was presiding over proceedings. Alistair looked every inch the Chief, dressed in the kilt, cloak and feathered bonnet, so I was disappointed that he spoke with an English public school accent. His family have held sway in nearby Ethie Castle for over 500 years but he now earns his living in London in the insurance business. As I stood with him drinking whisky by his tent he seemed distanced from the local community. He is a Scot at heart if not of hearth, and believes devolution will come.

'Not so much through any hatred of the English,' he explained, 'but because there is no sense of being properly represented at Westminster. Arbroath has high unemployment and the town feels neglected.'

It was a sentiment we've heard before, most notably on Eigg: people feel that they must take back responsibility for themselves to be able to best plan and fund future developments.

SANDI Inside the large tea-tent, two very ancient Calor gas cookers, which might have been plucked from some great aunt's kitchen, were bellowing away at fried onions and formerly frozen beef-burgers. Tea in plastic cups, which burn your hands before you get a mouthful, were trading fast. Beyond the tent flaps, the rain and the cabers came down.

POSTCARD NUMBER 10: *Modern image of Scotland (note the racy car).*

 ## Arbroath, the Farne Islands, Beadnell, Bamburgh

SHIP'S LOG: LIGHT WINDS, SEA STATE CALM.

SANDI We headed south, past Berwick-upon-Tweed and the Scottish border, towards the Farne Islands. Here a grey starling is supposed to have saved many a poor soul. I don't care how you get saved, I'm in favour of it. The injury to my hands leaves me more and more at the helm and less preoccupied with heaving canvas.

At first we stayed close to the coastline, enjoying the sights and imagining the smells of the fresh fields.

'Minke whale!' shouted Tom. We all rushed to see its tail flash, some 200 yards astern. These things never lose their delight.

Just before sunset, a peculiar bank of cloud appeared heading towards us. It was a curious thing. There was brilliant sunlight on one side and then a complete stripe of cloud from the sea up to 20 degrees in the sky. It was rather eerie as it marched inexorably towards us. When you watch the weather forecast on television they talk about approaching fronts: I just didn't know what they meant before. As John and I retired below to sleep, he asked Tom if the cloud might become a problem. He shrugged. We have all given up any form of prediction.

JOHN The sea was so gentle we hardly noticed the boat's motion as we lay on our bunks sipping whisky. It was so cosy in our cabin that we enjoyed quite a few furtive tots.

'One more for the road?' asked Sandi.

'There is no road,' I advised.

'I'll drink to that!' said the bundle of clothes in the rack above me. We did. I needed another drink myself. By the light of the small battery lamp, we lay reading. I was fascinated by John Cleese's book, *Families and How to Survive Them*, while Sandi was looking more directly at her own family. Brian had sent her a newly published book of her great-aunt Signe's diary from her days as a writer in Ireland.

We woke at 4.30 a.m. The fog had come in with a vengeance. The world was again reduced: a few hundred square yards of dark grey sea and cold, damp air.

'Farne Islands,' said Sandi. 'One of the most beautiful places in Britain.'

'Perhaps, but where are they?' I asked as we peered into the gloom.

We had planned to anchor at Lindisfarne to explore but that would have been impossible in these conditions. Out of the fog appeared a small open fishing boat

Hitching a lift.

with a very small wheelhouse at the front and an enormous wooden tiller at the high stern. Sandi and I hitched a lift.

The *Helen Esther* is a traditional flat-bottomed boat called a coble. Her high stern enables her to be pulled up and launched from a beach. She is 36 feet long but looked tiny. Tom held steady on his course while the skipper executed an impressive piece of seamanship. He came alongside and held his boat constantly just 2 feet from *Hirta*.

With no time to consider the matter, John and I jumped the 2-foot gap over the seas. That moment is forever crystallized in my mind. I can still feel myself in mid-air between two wooden boats in the middle of a fog and upset sea. We landed on top of the large wooden boxes where the fresh salmon are brought aboard. The fish oil ingrained in the wood caused us both to slide across the boat

and land in an unsteady and less than dignified manner. Fisherman John smiled and moved his boat away from *Hirta*.

I shook for about ten minutes afterwards, my heart pounding a furious version of Beethoven's *Fifth*. John, the skipper, was at the tiller wearing an ancient corduroy cap and oilskin smock, while Alfie, a dashing chap with a moustache, sorted out the nets. They had a passenger, Charlie Douglas, eighty-five with no teeth to speak of, a flat cap and a fisherman's smock. These familiar waters held no fear for them as they cheerfully steamed about in the thick conditions. Alfie stood talking to me. It was some time before I realized that nobody was speaking with a Scottish accent. We had arrived in England. The thick Northumberland accent was as impenetrable as the fog. It was a curious way to wake up.

JOHN We went off, as the fog started lifting, still unconscious how near or far land was. We watched the crew set their drift nets for salmon. Alfie played out the nets.

'Six hundred yards is the maximum allowed,' he explained as the net trimmed with white floats settled on the water behind us. Attached to the end of the net was an orange buoy surmounted with a red flag. Alfie threw it into the water. Once the nets were in position we began patrolling them.

John said that he plans to retire next year and doubts that anyone will get a licence from the Rivers Authority to fish in his place. He is a quietly-spoken man and I sensed a deep sadness in him at the passing of another traditional way of life. I suspect if I return, in five or six years, it will have passed away.

After half an hour Alfie hauled the net in via a large drum reminiscent of the old wringers on washing machines. It took a good ten minutes as water and bits of flotsam sprayed on to the deck. Alfie wore a baseball cap to avoid getting a jellyfish on his head. These are job difficulties which never normally cross my mind.

SANDI The Northumberland seal is a cheeky fellow and needs to be kept an eye on. The second we dropped the net an impudent young seal poked his head out of the water to see what was happening. For a seal, drift-net fishing is basically a free lunch. The salmon rather stupidly swim into the net and the seals just pull them out. John the skipper had dyed the net a rather lurid yellow colour. I would have thought even a myopic fish would see it coming, but apparently not. On the water's surface a pool of oil appeared, marking Sammy the Seal's lunch-spot.

We stood watching the salmon being landed. All we saw were their heads and half their bodies, just poking through the net as Alfie scooped up a piece of the long net and pulled the fish on board. In fairly swift succession four enormous salmon, absolutely beautiful-looking creatures, were pulled from the sea and placed in a blue plastic crate.

I couldn't help but feel distressed as the noble fish flapped around in the box. My father always hit fish on the head when he caught them but fisherman John explained that doing this causes the flesh to stiffen. The catch needs to be kept soft and pliable, so the fish are left to die in their own time. I was mesmerized by the vivid red behind the gills as they opened and closed in desperate gasps for life. Two salmon were landed together.

Fisherman John looked at them. 'Must have been swimming together,' he laughed. 'Perhaps they were a salmon couple.'

He shouldn't have said it. People react so emotionally to the humanization of the animal world. Give a piece of venison a tricky childhood and it becomes Bambi, endearing and utterly unedible. The temptation to pick the fish up out of the box and throw them back into the sea was almost unbearable but we were guests. I don't think I'd have been very popular if I'd liberated their day's catch. I know I was being hypocritical. I felt guilty. I adore salmon. I love eating. I just don't want to watch my food dying or suffering in any way. Supermarkets have divorced us from the reality of what we are eating. I'm sure most kids think meat is made shrink-wrapped.

As we approached Beadnell harbour, we could see three old boys in an open wooden rowing boat, salmon-fishing off the beach from staked nets. An incredibly old chap was rowing the boat with two companions. They had been hard at work, hauling in nets and dropping them again, all morning and had caught precisely one salmon. It was hard to imagine that this could still be a living. We were witnessing the last legacy of a bygone era.

The coble is stationed in Beadnell, a tiny harbour on the Northumberland coast. It has the distinction of being the only west-facing harbour on the entire east coast. It is a really snug little place with wide stone walls and great sagging bits where the stone has just collapsed under the strain of sitting there all those years. Outside the enclosed harbour, ranks of twin-keeled yachts stood on the drained beach facing out to sea.

JOHN I wandered up from the harbour with Charlie Douglas and met his brother Tom outside their old, tar-painted fishing huts. Charlie is the younger brother at eighty-five; Tom is three years his senior. They could have been teenagers, mercilessly teasing each other, indeed everyone, all the time. They told me outrageous tales of their life as fishermen. At least, I think they did. From within their broad Northumbrian accents and dialect I picked up some of the yarns about

battles with neighbouring fishing communities and the rivalry over fishing skills, still fiercely contested. They scorned mention of radar and electronic fish-finders.

While we were talking another old fellow appeared, shouting at us to get off his land. 'Tell him to bugger off!' Charlie muttered to me while Tom shouted and laughed at the newcomer. It turned out that the intruder was another brother with whom they had been feuding. Charlie had not spoken to him for years. The cause of this family rift remained a mystery.

I felt out of place and insubstantial sitting with them in jeans and a shirt while they wore dark heavy trousers and jackets and cloth caps, above faces that seemed etched with ancient wisdom. They were not maudlin but full of vitality, full of certainty that their life had been worthwhile.

Fisherman John appeared with his guitar and a friend who played the Northumbrian pipes. Their lyrical music formed a perfect background as I looked out at the sea and the old huts where Charlie, Tom and their brothers had spent their lives mending their nets and tending their boats. It is sad to think that when they die, so too will their way of life.

By late afternoon we ended up in Bamburgh, the main local village. There was no doubt that we were no longer in Scotland. The undulation in the fields and the climbing roses on the cottage walls tell you in no uncertain terms that

OPPOSITE:
Beadnell harbour.

*Our first English
accents for weeks.*

this is England. United in one kingdom but, architecturally at least, divided into quite separate countries.

Bamburgh Castle is an enormous pile leaping straight out of rock. We've seen so many old castles built on great rock promontories that I wonder if architectural schools of the time ran special courses in rock foundation. The fog had lifted and from the battlements we could at last see the previously shy Farne Islands. In the distance lay Holy Island, home of Lindisfarne, the famous religious community.

In the early evening John and I took a walk along the beach. We weren't working; we weren't writing or travelling or meeting new people.

'We'll be home in a month,' said John.

'Let's take our shoes off,' I replied.

It was the first time we could feel the pleasures of the coast. Rather than just going around it, we were actually walking on it and enjoying it.

SAFETY TIP
If a thunderstorm strikes when you are on the beach,
the safest place to be is behind a sand dune.

DAY 53 Bamburgh

I have not been able to get my hands warm. The swelling is worse than ever. I have been told to rest them – impossible while we are still on the journey. Just three weeks and two days to go. I will have to scale down the amount of work I can do on board. We are to meet up with *Hirta* tomorrow; today, we rest.

We strolled across the green at Bamburgh to the Grace Darling Museum. Grace Darling was a late-nineteenth-century heroine. She was the daughter of the Farne Island lighthouse-keeper and is supposed to have rowed with her father to save nine crew off the *Forfarshire* steamer as she went down. Grace got most of the credit and became enough of a Victorian superstar to be offered money to row a mechanized boat across the stage at Drury Lane. Nice to know that standards in show business have never changed. Grace is still a bit of an industry around Bamburgh. John viewed the coble she'd rowed while I bought a rubber with her picture on it. Having been through the fog around here, I think she's a heroine.

DAY 54 Blyth to Whitby

SHIP'S LOG: WIND NORTH-EASTERLY FORCE 3 OR 4,
SEA STATE CALM.

We rejoined *Hirta* at Blyth, where a line of futuristic windmills waved us off from the yacht club (which boasts the oldest yacht clubhouse in the country), at the unusually civilized time of 9 in the morning. A favourable wind pulled us along past the smoking chimneys of Newcastle and Hartlepool. *Hirta*'s tan sails look timeless against the blue sea and sky. Perfect cruising weather and another welcome shot of the addictive sailing drug. Sandi, sadly, is having to take more conventional medicine; her hands are badly swollen and ache from too much strain. She is very despondent that she cannot heave ropes or do any knotting until she is better. Maybe she can concentrate on navigation.

I'm pretty much useless now as a member of the crew. I got no sleep at all last night from the pain and swelling in my hands and the pills I've been given upset my stomach. I had got used to being a functioning member of the crew and to no longer be of much use is extremely depressing. I do battle with the condition every minute. I will not appear weak, having come this far. John is kind and solicitous but I am bad-tempered with myself. I am so conscious of having been a woman in a man's world and I don't want to go girlie now. I try to 'be of the moment' and am at least heartened today by the sunshine and the calm seas. They give sailing a completely different feel.

When part of your body refuses to play, it makes you realize how powerless you are over the physical dimensions of your own life. I do so want not to be unfit. I sat and looked at the sea and thought of the ocean within. A woman my size has about 30 pints of salt water running about in her body. Roughly three-quarters of this is plasma, the watery bit of blood, and the rest is intestinal fluid. We are flooded by the sea and can no more control it than the wind and the waves.

JOHN It was the most peaceful and pleasant day's sail we have had on the whole trip. The sun warmed us on deck and lit up the towns and rolling hills along this very English coastline. Oddly, we slept most of the time. If not steering, cooking or attending to ropes, people tiptoed around until a likely-looking spot was found for a good doze. I don't know if this was because we are exhausted or if we were just letting ourselves be lulled by the hope that the rest of the journey will be as sublime as it is at the moment. I was surprised that I could sleep as I find it hard to ignore peripheral sounds; a hangover, I think, from captivity.

WHITBY

In its time, Whitby was a great whaling port. As early as 1825, the streets of Whitby were lit by gas made from whale oil produced by boiling blubber on the quayside. William Scoresby, famous whaling captain and inventor of the crow's-nest, sailed from here. He caught 533 whales in his time, which is obviously more than most people.

SANDI There is an incredibly narrow entrance to Whitby pier, framed by proper British seaside paraphernalia. The place was absolutely packed with holiday-makers and fish and chip shops cheek by jowl with bingo halls. Strings of lights cast a coloured glow over the town as amateur fishermen called greetings to us from the great stone walls beneath a small lighthouse. We steered our way in under full sail, each of us feeling a certain pride in the snatched photos and remarks from pointing holiday-makers. Steering is about the only thing I can do now. I kept a firm eye on the stone walls on either side; I know about audiences. We'd gathered a big crowd and I didn't want to mess up now. The gigantic iron swing-bridge allowed us through into a well-protected harbour. Along the wall, a single string of white lights lit up the streets and were reflected in the water. It was all beginning to feel less like a long job and more like an adventure. We knew we'd arrived in Yorkshire when we spotted a yacht called *Ay Up*.

55 Whitby

The old town of Whitby lies on the south side of the River Esk, with narrow, winding cobbled streets and 199 steep stone steps running up to the church and ruined abbey on the cliff above. On the cliffs above the north side of the harbour are more recent Georgian and Victorian buildings, most of which are

Whitby harbour.

now hotels or guest houses with that atmosphere of genteel decay which is typical of so many British resorts. A cunning entrepreneur must lie behind the charges on the beach lift. It costs five pence more to come up from the brightly coloured bathing huts than it does to go down.

I couldn't help feeling homesick, walking along the front beside families splashing each other in paddling pools and encouraging Grandad at the clock golf. Everything was safe, secure and predictable. It may have lacked adventure but it was rich with simple pleasures. The seasoned traveller in me had to fight hard to overcome an urge to buy a kiss-me-quick hat and I compromised with a full-blown fish and chip lunch down by the harbour. Whitby's tourism lives alongside its fishing industry – the fleet of twenty or so boats tied up along the north harbour wall beside the fish market sheds, just across the street from the row of much-used amusement arcades.

 Whitby is absolutely packed with holiday-makers and I think the largest collection of tattoos that I've seen anywhere – both on men and on women. More on men than on women. The men have also cornered the market in beer-bellies. I think the British are not necessarily the most attractive race in the world when they holiday, but then any man who thinks he looks attractive in shell-suit fabric shorts and no shirt needs to be advised differently.

I had been commissioned to get some groceries but I hate shopping and am easily distracted. A string of tourists passed clutching furry footballs and cuddly toys from amusement arcades – a succession of teddies whose eyes are destined to fall out the second they reach home. From one of the amusement arcades I could hear a woman calling out the eccentric nicknames for the numbers which came up. 'Legs eleven' I was familiar with but why is nine 'doctors' orders' or ten 'one lying in the road'? I had no idea. I couldn't resist having a go myself. Bingo has changed since the days when it was played in church halls and people crossed out numbers on a card. The new thing is highly organized and mechanized. The number cards are permanently illuminated at each seat and the caller has an electronic device behind the desk which enables her to tell immediately who's got a bingo. In fact I worked out that you could put your money into the machine and just sit there. You didn't actually have to pay any attention but I think shouting out 'Bingo!' at the relevant moment is all part of it. If you don't it rather takes the fun away.

Not that people were necessarily there for fun. You can still win a ceramic pen-holder shaped like a poodle but most people are there for the groceries. I sat next to a woman who'd got a caravan near Whitby. Her family always come here for their holidays and she goes to the bingo with three pounds. If she doesn't win then she doesn't play any more but the secret, she confided, is to take food vouchers if you win. I had never heard of people playing bingo for food. In my day bingo meant Catholics in church halls getting as close to sin as they dared, but that was the past. Now you can exchange your wins for vouchers at the Presto supermarket or Marks and Spencer's. My new companion told me that a friend of hers had won the jackpot recently and ended up with twenty-five pounds' worth of food at Presto's. Now she was happily spending much of her break trying to win the groceries for her family's weekend.

Surrounded by dedicated women players, I did rather well for a novice-run, with five wins including a three-win on my gold card. I scorned the his-and-her condiment sets shaped like pigs, the turquoise dustpans and brushes, furry dice and depressed toilet-roll holders and took home three tins of soup, three tins of baked beans, a large packet of tea-bags and a giant bar of fruit and nut chocolate. I asked my new chum if any of the men ever came down to play and she chuckled at the notion. This was definitely a woman's game, best played in a floral print dress, preferably from a catalogue.

JOHN While Sandi lurked in the amusement arcades I joined the Cunliffes for a trip round the bay in an old lifeboat. The *Mary-Ann Hepworth* served between 1938 and 1974, saving 201 lives. She's now owned by Barry whose long grey locks, slightly portly frame and garrulous nature made me think of Ronnie Biggs. I wasn't surprised when he said: 'I'm lead guitar in a heavy metal band at weekends'. Since being diagnosed as a diabetic he can no longer serve in the RNLI so he runs the old boat for tourists. Although full of patter, the way Barry keeps her brasses and woodwork shining shows his love for the valiant old craft and the crews who served on her. Tom was delighted to find out that *Hirta*'s engine is the same type as that of the *Mary-Ann*. He and Barry became excited over the possibility that a carpenter, who once worked on *Hirta*, had served his apprenticeship in the Southampton yard where the *Mary-Ann* was built.

SANDI Whitby is reputed to be the most haunted place in Britain. The author, Bram Stoker, set scenes of his novel *Dracula* on the long flight of steps which meander up through the old town to the graveyard and church of St Mary, not to mention the ruined abbey, on the East Cliff.

In the evening we had a date with the Count. Well, it's a living, isn't it? Up on the cliffs of Whitby, beside an arch made from whalebone, we met Rex Greenwood, who gives his Dracula performance nightly. He stood in full Dracula regalia attracting quite a lot of attention. Tom, Ros and Hannah sat on a bench nearby as if it was absolutely nothing to do with them. I have rarely seen so much stage make-up in daylight outside an open-air performance of *The Boy Friend*.

Rex used to be a mining engineer but he's been playing Dracula on and off for twenty-nine years. For twelve years he did the same show four nights a week at the Royal Hotel. Obviously a man of some perseverance. He was completely transfixed by the story of Dracula and told us it is the best-selling book after the Bible and the *Guinness Book of Records*. What that tells us about people's reading habits in this country I've absolutely no idea.

Bram Stoker had been standing, looking out of the window – probably at the Royal Hotel – when a boat called *The Dimeta* had become shipwrecked, with the dead captain allegedly lashed to the wheel of the boat. Old Bram Stoker saw a dog escape from the wreckage on to the beach below East Cliff and run up the 199 steps to a man sitting on a bench. This, said Rex, obviously gave him the idea for Dracula. I didn't get the link myself but then I can never think of any answer when journalists ask me 'Where do you get your ideas from?'

The Cunliffes were unimpressed and went back to the boat.

HELPING HAND

The local museum gives pride of place to a murderer's wizened hand which was severed at the wrist after his execution. The hand was used for years as a charm by burglars and was believed to have the power to send victims into a deep slumber. A similar effect to going on a long sail.

Chris, Paul and Charles, three local musicians, came aboard for a drink. An impromptu music session was soon underway. As Chris played his own composition, 'Golden Grove', on the accordion, his friends picked up the tune and the saloon was filled with the lilting melody conjuring up balmy sea voyages. Tom and Ros loved the tune, saying it reminded them, quite precisely, of sailing in a fair wind. The musicians played a number of reels and jigs as we drank beers in the soft light of the oil lamps. Everyone became very relaxed, especially Sandi.

'Do you do requests?' she asked and, encouraged by a positive reply from the band, demanded 'March of the Toreadors' from *Carmen*. The tune sounded slightly out of place on fiddle, guitar and squeeze-box but the bravura performance did not entirely satisfy Sandi.

'Let's all sing "Wonderful, Wonderful Copenhagen".'

We did, and rounded off a splendid evening.

The North Sea

SHIP'S LOG: VARIABLE LIGHT WINDS,
SEA STATE CALM.

JOHN In 1768 Captain James Cook left Whitby in the *Endeavour* to sail to Tahiti. We set sail at 11 a.m. for Great Yarmouth. At the fuel berth a surly character seemed loath to sell us diesel. Our faith in Whitby's friendliness was restored when we saw last night's accordion player, Chris, and his girlfriend waving us off from the pier and then heard Barry wish us a loud, crackly enthusiastic 'bon voyage' over the lifeboat's megaphone.

SANDI The sun shone and, with her topsail up, *Hirta* looked resplendent under full canvas. Quite a lot of sleeping went on in the afternoon. Everybody was feeling a little the worse for wear but there wasn't a problem sharing out the steering and the various jobs to be done on board. For the first time it was decided that John and I would take a night-watch on our own. He and I would do from 10 until midnight and then Ros, Hannah and Tom would each take a watch. This gave everyone short two-hour watches and six hours' kip. Practically a holiday.

John and cameraman, Alex Hansen, poised for action in the frenetic world of long-distance sailing.

JOHN At ten o'clock, alone on the deck, Sandi and I were very tense. Gradually we relaxed as we realized that we had lights twinkling reassuringly on the land off to the west, and that with very little cloud to obscure the light of the moon and stars we could be confident of being able to keep a watch for other ships. There is a pleasant intimacy in sharing a night-watch on a boat: the hushed consultations and the solidarity of joint decisions. We sailed down past Hull, where I first met Sandi's brother Nick in our university days. We could see a lot of traffic going into Grimsby as we strained to keep an eye on all the movement around us.

SANDI This was a proper night-watch, unlike the one across Liverpool Bay, where very little happened. There are a large number of gas fields off the eastern coast and boats are required by law to keep an exclusion zone of 500 metres. Visibility was good and we could see the gas fields a long way off, the sun setting against their flared towers in an earthenware glow. It looked like some strange Aztec or Mayan village rising up in the distance. By the time darkness fell the fields were a blaze of white light and they had changed personality into something much more modern, much more Battleship Galactica. John and I were resolute in our diligence. It is a fearful feeling to be utterly in charge while everyone else sleeps. We took turns steering and being on watch, checking shipping with the binoculars.

JOHN The night lit up as we passed through the gas fields; the rigs looked like tower blocks in the ocean. There was activity all around them; supply and maintenance vessels moved in and out. We felt like country cousins lost in the big

Teamwork.

179

city where all manner of sophisticated operations were underway beyond our understanding. Suddenly we noticed a light flashing on one of the guard boats.

'What's that?' I wondered.

'Don't know,' said Sandi at the helm. 'Shall we put the hand-held radio on?'

'Good idea. Where is it?'

I located the radio and tuned to the open VHF channel for the area. It crackled into life.

'Yacht passing to the east of the gas field, this is Blue Flame 1.'

'Are we east?' asked Sandi.

I nodded. 'Must be us.' I pressed the talk button. 'Blue Flame 1, this is yacht *Hirta*. Are you calling us?'

'Just checking someone's on watch and awake.'

'Fine, thanks.'

'OK, then. Have a good trip.'

Sandi and I grinned. We really were running the boat. Blue Flame 1 would never have guessed it was our first night-watch. It was such a delight to be making practical decisions on our own as we sheeted in the banging mainsail slightly to avoid waking our resting companions.

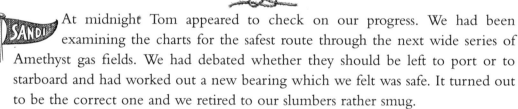

At midnight Tom appeared to check on our progress. We had been examining the charts for the safest route through the next wide series of Amethyst gas fields. We had debated whether they should be left to port or to starboard and had worked out a new bearing which we felt was safe. It turned out to be the correct one and we retired to our slumbers rather smug.

'Well done, John,' I said as we settled down to sleep.

'Well done, you,' he replied.

Those two hours of night-watch were some of the best of the entire trip.

DAY 57 Norfolk Coast to Great Yarmouth

I slept soundly until 6.30 a.m. and woke to find the cabin was already filled with brightness from the prismatic glass lights in the deck above me. Sandi had been in the pipe cot when I went to sleep but I now found her on the saloon floor – she had not been able to sleep in her cramped rack.

I clambered over her and went on deck to find Tom and Ros on watch enjoying the sunshine. Once again the landscape had changed. With the full complement of sails we were racing along the low Norfolk coastline past buoys carefully marking the sandbanks and shoals which bear the splendid name of The Scrobies. Tom briefed us on our duties for dropping the sails and mooring up once we were in Great Yarmouth harbour.

 The pilot book is not terribly enthusiastic about Great Yarmouth. I had thought yacht pilot books were meant to give you safety and mooring instructions but this one was critical on aesthetic grounds. It says Great Yarmouth is one of the ugliest places you could hope to come in, and that really neither the harbour nor the town has anything to recommend it.

It is certainly a curious place – a very narrow entrance and then a sharp turn to the right and up what looks basically like a canal for miles and miles. We might almost have been coming in to Copenhagen as we sailed several miles up a canal, passing old maritime buildings with the kind of roof construction that guards against the snows of Scandinavia.

There were tankers all over the place and although space was tight, everything went well. Apart from bringing the topsail down. It's well-named. It sits at the top of the mast and it is always a bit scary when it comes down because it is unsupported and extremely heavy. It weighs the equivalent of a normal yacht's mainsail – about 150 pounds – and it just comes straight down at you. One of the ropes controlling the topsail had become stuck high up by the mast. Ros effortlessly climbed the ratlines (the rope ladder in the shrouds) and managed to yank it free. I took it in my arms and John very kindly assisted me in holding it. Just when we think we have learnt something, our inexperience taps us on the shoulder. At this point he accidentally let go of the main halyard. I felt terrible. If he hadn't been helping me it might not have happened.

 I watched helplessly as the weight of the rope carried the shackle inexorably up to the very top of the mast; where it stuck. We could not set sail again until someone retrieved it and I knew it was going to be me. I'd let it go, I would have to shin up the mast and get it down. I had never ventured far up the shrouds, let alone stepped above them. Setting off on the first few rungs I was overwhelmed by nerves. I could not imagine how Ros had made the climb look so easy; the ratlines were so far apart. But the shame of giving up and leaving someone else to rectify my mistake outweighed physical fear and I continued. Our cameraman Alex had often been up the ratlines to film, so he fitted me out with his safety harness. He talked me through every step.

Unused to the unaccustomed strain on my muscles I soon began to run out of stamina. As I neared the top of the ratlines, Alex called out: 'Attach your harness to that bolt by your hand … on the mast. Let it take your weight, then you can rest for a minute.'

I took his advice and felt a surge of confidence as I realized that I was secure and that at worst I might slip and bruise myself against the mast. I looked down and saw Tom, Ros and Hannah smiling encouragement and Alex, lying flat on the deck, watching me through his binoculars: they seemed a very long way below me.

With my nose up against the mast I inched my way aloft to within 5 or 6 feet of the top, which was as far as I could usefully go. Tom hauled a hook made from a coat-hanger up to me, and on the second attempt, I caught the wretched shackle and, with one hand still firmly around the mast, pulled it down to me with the other, clamping the halyard between my teeth. Within a minute, to the cheers of my shipmates, Ros was making the shackle fast in its rightful place.

I clambered back down to the deck with arms and legs shaking from the physical and nervous exertion. Alex was beaming at me and I felt much love and gratitude for him. It was a huge relief to have put things right and I was delighted to have overcome my initial terror. When I had calmed down, I remembered again Ros's agile climb earlier in the afternoon and the times I had watched Alex not only climb the mast but operate a camera while up there. Mine was no great feat, but I was delighted to have done it.

DAY 58 Great Yarmouth

 We thought we'd hit seaside proper with Whitby, but Great Yarmouth is the whole event gone mad. I avoided The Shipwreck Experience. They've spent one-and-a-half million pounds re-creating some of the finest shipwrecks in the world. Not my idea of a good time.

We've still got hundreds of miles to travel. I went to find out if we were going to make it. Fortune-telling is as integral a part of the British seaside as knotted hankies and sunburnt noses. I had mine told by a very old chap called Bert who said he was seventy-seven. Certainly his suit was about that age: a limp effort over a brown V-neck pullover, frayed at the edges with a menu of past meals displayed down the front. Bert had clearly shrunk over

OPPOSITE: *Another bowsprit moment.* the years and now wore his shirt collar like

some loose equine-restraining device. Bert was very intense about my £2.30 reading and it took rather a long time. The gist of it seems to be that I am very lucky and might one day open a garden centre. I'm thrilled to bits.

Sandi returned from having her fortune told, wittering on about bulbs and biennials which sat oddly with the fancy cap she wore at a rakish angle with the word 'Captain' emblazoned above the brim.

'If you behave yourself tomorrow I might let you wear this,' she informed me. Her confidence in me was to prove misplaced.

DAY 59   Great Yarmouth and the Norfolk Broads

It was my idea so I've only got myself to blame. I said 'Great Yarmouth is so close to the Broads, why don't we go sailing there?' The mistake was to say it when one of the others was listening.

We drove inland, heading for the Waveney Boatyard at Burgh St Peter where we'd hired a boat for the day. A sweet little thing; 30 feet long, with a fibreglass hull, but a wooden superstructure, called *Lydia*. Her rig was pleasingly familiar – throat halyard, peak halyard and so on.

With great zeal I started to pull up the mainsail. The boom rolled out of the sail and dropped with a thud on the fancy 'Captain' hat which was, sadly, still on Sandi's head. I felt terrible: about to embark on our first solo voyage I had concussed my shipmate with a pitifully elementary error. Sandi took refuge in the little cabin and I followed her in.

'I'm so sorry.' I hugged her. 'Are you all right?'

She managed a weak smile through her tears. 'Well, I'm not giving up now.'

After a very short time she decided she was fit enough to carry on.

Our producer, Jeremy, had decided that we should really test ourselves and go it alone but, following my unprovoked attack on Sandi, he allowed Tom to run through some basic instructions. As we cast off he shouted that they would be waiting for us a few miles down the Waveney river, then added, 'Remember, the big problem is not moving but stopping!'

The moment we started moving away from the quay and turned downstream we looked at each other with an appalling realization: we were responsible for this craft and we did not know what to do. Everything that we had learnt in two months aboard *Hirta* evaporated in a mist of panic. Tom had shown us how the sails generated power with the wind and we were used to tacking, hauling sheets, holding a course, but we had never made a decision about that course or the set of the sails ourselves.

SANDI While John concentrated on the sails I took up the helm. Unlike the steering wheel on *Hirta*, *Lydia* had a tiller. If you wanted to go left, you had to move it to the right. I continuously muttered to myself: 'Go in the opposite direction to the one you want. Go in the opposite direction to the one you want'. I kept saying it to myself but, without question, Tiller the Hun was very likely going to be the undoing of us. At least John seemed to have a very good hang of the ropes and sheets.

JOHN I experimented letting the sails out and then pulling them in. The boat did not respond, and I hadn't a clue why. Sandi and I were building up oceans of resentment against the silent Jeremy who obstinately refused to share any of his own sailing experience as he sat in the cabin directing the filming. There are times when the camera becomes nothing but a mocking evil-eye; you want to scream at it: 'So you know everything, do you? You think I'm pretty bloody stupid, don't you? Try it yourself, you smug, conceited etc. etc'.

Fortunately, a motor boat was following at a discreet distance with the second camera-crew on board. One of them, a keen yachtsman and a kind soul, took pity and mimed that I should haul in the mainsail. I did so and *Lydia* took off. I sheeted in the jib and we started cruising pleasantly along. Filled with soaring confidence, Sandi and I hugged each other and laughed dismissively at the evil-eye.

With the initial panic over we were able to think more clearly and realized that we would have to adjust the sails often to cope with the changes in wind direction as we went around the bends in the river. We managed a number of turns successfully and peace descended as we cruised along gently, listening to the water burbling under our bow and the wind rustling the reeds on the bank.

SANDI We got quite excited as we sped along, feeling rather superior to other holiday-makers in their motor boats. The tide was with us and, with the wind behind us, we were cracking along, maybe doing 3 or 4 knots. It seemed to be going extremely well. It was almost too easy.

OVERLEAF: *Talking train timetables.*

185

As we got the hang of this we felt that we must have learnt a lot on *Hirta* after all and that this solo experience was all we had needed to make us master mariners. Jeremy, however, decided it was too straightforward.

'I want you to go about and head upriver,' he ordered.

This was absurd. We'd be going against the tide.

We did as we were told. Now, sailing was a completely different matter. The wind was right on the nose. The only way to keep moving was to close-haul the boat and make short tacks across the narrow river. It wasn't easy.

'We need to tack,' Sandi said to me.

'We can't,' I replied.

'Why not?'

'There's a cameraman on the jib.'

Picture the scene – you're a fledgling sailor in charge of your first boat, trying to sail into the wind. Standing directly in your way is a large cameraman and an even larger soundman with a mini producer shouting orders from inside the cabin. Dead ahead of you, as you try to tack round, is a large motorized camera boat with more people watching your every move and capturing your every expletive. In my defence, I did call to the other boat to please get out of the way but the message was relayed, I feel, without the required haste. I could see the motor boat dead ahead. There seemed to be nothing I could do about it. I pushed the tiller very hard one way – clearly, the wrong way – and smack, bam, our bowsprit rammed straight into the camera-boat with a thundering judder. I do not feel I can be entirely blamed. Hitting the reeds later, however, was almost totally down to me.

Sandi put the tiller hard over and *Lydia* turned sweetly, almost within her own length. But the collision had shattered our concentration and the boat seemed to have developed a mind of her own. We tried to keep clear of the reeds which lined the bank but *Lydia* had other ideas and we ploughed into them. We started the engine but she refused to back away into the stream. Gingerly I lowered myself off the bow and, though sinking a foot into the mud, got enough purchase to shove her off and we headed off once more. Or would have done but for a momentary lapse of wheel-steering mentality and going the wrong way with the tiller: thus achieving intimacy with the reeds on the other bank as well.

We were at one with nature and I couldn't stop laughing. We had a go at reversing out with the engine but the sweet little thing had no intention of being helpful. John rolled up his trousers and got into the mud again. He assured me it was still very black and very sticky, but put up a fine effort as he eased us back into the stream. Marvellous chap. Perhaps we should have swapped places but John seemed to know so much more about the sails, so I left him to it.

Confident that we had been through the worst, we rounded a corner and found a swing-bridge, which wasn't swung, directly across our path. By now I was blubbing with laughter. We survived our wait for the bridge and before we knew it, the pub, The Bell Inn where we were to meet Tom, was literally around the corner. We should have just gone for it but we decided to practise mooring out of sight so we wouldn't embarrass ourselves when we arrived.

A wall on the far bank looked like the perfect place to rehearse. Sandi took us about perfectly and I positioned the fenders ready for the light bump as we came alongside the wall. Sadly, and very unexpectedly, the wall had its own fendering system: mud. Three feet away from the wall *Lydia* grounded. We shifted the tiller, flapped the sails and moved our weight around the boat but to no avail. Now the propeller was in the mud. The rudder was in the mud. We were about as jammed into the mud as you can get.

There was general mumbled agreement that it wasn't my fault this time. That I had turned the right way and no one could have predicted there would be mud there. It didn't help to get us out but I felt better.

A large motor boat steamed towards us. On board I could see two nice young lads wearing Jewish yarmulke on the back of their heads.

'Oh, good,' I said to John. 'Nice lads, they'll help us off.'

'Will you tow us off?' I called.

'No,' they said, turned the corner and buggered off. So much for the etiquette of the waterways and so much for people wearing their religion on their sleeves.

'Your mothers would be ashamed,' I yelled.

The camera-boat, which had gone on ahead, returned and we suffered the indignity of being pulled off by a boat we'd previously rammed. Down at the St Olave and Johnson boatyard, we were confronted with a lot of moored boats and a fixed bridge cutting off any escape. Plus the Cunliffes were all watching. After one aborted attempt we made the mooring under engine-power. It had been a baptism of fire.

I'd like to think the crack on the head had stopped my brain functioning but the fact is the tiller did me in. Indeed, at one point John just grabbed it off me and pushed it the other way to avoid yet another beckoning river bank. John says that next time I'm getting in the mud. Seems reasonable.

JOHN We sat in *Lydia*'s cockpit and had a beer to celebrate our qualified success. Tom was delighted that we had managed with reasonable dignity and laughed at our disasters, telling us that it was from this very boatyard that he had first sailed as a fourteen-year-old. Three minutes into that journey, he'd dropped an important shackle overboard.

'You always get these disasters when you're learning,' he said comfortingly.

In a 5-mile voyage we had hit the bank twice, rammed another boat and run aground. These disasters I could accept as part of the learning curve but I was still haunted by my hitting Sandi over the head with a large piece of wood.

'I still feel bad,' I told her.

'I am a bit shaky,' she confided. 'I expect you'll have to come with me to play the machines tonight.'

I felt I had to. Devious swine.

THAT EVENING

SANDI As the sun set, the front at Great Yarmouth looked as much like a tacky postcard version of Las Vegas as you can manage on the east coast of Britain. Passing a woman holding a giant python on the pavement, we went to try our luck in the noisy amusement arcades.

'Let's try this,' exclaimed John, actually getting enthusiastic about the outing.

I warned him off. No one ever wins anything on those machines where you try to manoeuvre a metal claw to win a prize.

John instantly won a doll of Gomez from the Addams Family. He had thrown down a gauntlet. We could not depart until I had secured Gomez's partner, Mortitia. My head said the thing was rigged but my heart was determined. Proving much more adept at steering a crane than a boat, I at last had success. We were triumphant.

'Where shall we keep them on the boat?' I asked him as we clutched Mortitia and Gomez.

'In the shrouds, of course,' he replied.

We tried our luck elsewhere and ended up with forty-one prize-winning tickets. These I exchanged for two miniature football rattles and a plastic game of snakes and ladders. As I collected my prizes I noticed a large sign on the back of the cash register. It offered a free daily service by the police to have your children tagged so they might be easily identified if they became lost. It is a real sign of the times. Everywhere we have travelled in this country, everyone is focused on one thing – the safety of children. People in the small island communities constantly tell you that their children are safe. It is the main boast of the isolated areas. There is an

190

undercurrent of fear and concern for all kids in this country which can't be good for the grown-ups and certainly can't be much fun for the kids. Tagged kids at the seaside. Some holiday.

Great Yarmouth to Dover

SHIP'S LOG: LIGHT VARIABLE WINDS.

SANDI Overnight, a replica of *The Golden Hind* tied up behind us. Those old galleon boats are always much smaller than you expect for the voyages they made. It was lovely to see her proud shape with great yellow and black paintwork.

SIR FRANCIS DRAKE

The first Englishman to circumnavigate the globe. Our trip would have seemed like a weekend jaunt to him. *The Golden Hind*'s voyage round the world took 'two years, ten months and some few odde daies beside', as the old sea-dog wrote in his journal. His contribution in repelling the Spanish Armada gave him everlasting fame. He was somewhat helped by his opponents. It is said that the Spanish Navy in that battle had the worst aim in history. It fired 100 000 cannonballs at the English ships without scoring a single significant hit.

JOHN Tom had planned our passage from Great Yarmouth to Ramsgate very carefully to ensure that we got as much help as possible from the tides, to get us past the Thames estuary and its shoals. Looking at the charts I saw a large number of WK notations.

'Stands for wreck,' said Tom, confirming my fears.

We went on without mishap, following the buoys across the estuary towards the western tip of Kent at North Foreland. As we came down towards Margate we could see the wide cliffs on the northern face of Kent. Tom's reading of the tides had been so astute that we were off Ramsgate by half past four, much earlier than even he had dared to hope, so we decided to press on for a glorious sail past Broadstairs and Deal, towards Dover.

As we rounded South Foreland and entered the English Channel, the busiest seaway in the world, we toasted the start of the last leg of our journey to Falmouth with Champagne and wished for fair winds to ensure our arrival there in two weeks' time. At Tom's behest, Sandi anointed *Hirta*'s bowsprit with a drop or two of bubbly to acknowledge her stalwart efforts for us.

SANDI It was a happy day, with everyone in shorts, playing Scrabble in the cockpit. For a great deal of the time on the journey there had been absolutely nothing to see; just water all around us and no particular traffic. It was as we approached the Kent coast that this had begun to change. An Allsorts packet of tankers and tugs seemed to have been emptied on to the seas. Yachts, out enjoying a day's sailing, reappeared for the first time in weeks. We hadn't seen any in the north. The sea was lovely, the wind less than a force 2 and, as the sun slowly set, the famous white cliffs announced our arrival in Dover.

Dover has two entrances to the harbour – east and west – and you have to apply for permission to enter one as you approach. Over the radio we could hear foreign vessels calling in broken English for instructions. The place was a Piccadilly Circus of activity and we were approaching fast. We heard a ferry asking for permission to leave and we radioed Harbour Control explaining that we were three or four minutes away under sail and asking permission to proceed. In fact it took four-and-a-half minutes for us to reach the stone wall of the west entrance while Harbour Control held back a huge P&O ferry. Quite something.

JOHN We reached Dover at 7 o'clock, having made the 105-mile passage from Great Yarmouth in just fourteen hours. Tom rounded *Hirta* smartly up to a buoy as we dropped the foresails. As soon as we were in, the harbour patrol boat came alongside and led us to a mooring. There's too much going on in Dover Harbour to allow people to drift around.

SANDI For 2000 years Dover has been Britain's main cross-Channel port. It's one of those ports that people tend to pass through. You don't think about the people who actually live here. Lovely old, probably Georgian, buildings line the bay. It was a splendid vista until we noticed a great sweep of modern post-industrial flats. A Prince Charles carbuncle on the face of the port. Who makes these planning decisions?

'The physician can bury his mistakes, but the architect can only advise his clients to plant vines.'

FRANK LLOYD WRIGHT

DAY 61

Dover

SANDI There used to be a control tower on either side of the harbour but the eastern one was destroyed in the 1987 hurricane and never rebuilt. Odd to think that they needed it before but they don't need it now. Up in the western tower, two chaps, Derek and Josh, were busy controlling. They sat at a large desk of impressive equipment, fielding radio calls and watching the traffic pass below their windows. Television screens gave detailed images of both harbour entrances as well as the harbour itself. The stream of noise was constant but they seemed very relaxed as they easily distinguished what was directed at them and what was not.

A number of Dutch boats were arriving. 'A Dutchman is a Frenchman lying down,' Derek explained as he pointed out their flag and fielded a call in poor English.

'What happens if a foreign boat comes in and they give you a name that you don't quite get the handle of?' I asked him.

He shrugged and smiled. 'Oh, we just try and make a noise back that sounds the same.'

Beyond the eastern entrance we could see the spoils from the Channel Tunnel. Both Derek and Josh were rather sniffy about it as they handled the departure of three ferries within five minutes of each other. They felt the tunnel would never really take off.

A WELCOME BREAK

If you leave for France, one of the greatest culinary countries in the world, from Dover Harbour, the only place to get something to eat is somewhere called 'Welcome Break'. It isn't.

JOHN I always feel nervous going through Customs so I was delighted to have the opportunity to stand at the side of the law while travellers drove through the Customs Shed at Dover. I couldn't help feeling a certain thrill when the young officer I was shadowing, Tara, stopped a car that she thought was suspicious. The young driver got out.

'I've already been searched by the French Customs,' he exploded. 'Why am I being persecuted?' He spotted me standing behind Tara. 'God, they haven't got you as well, have they?'

Dover Docks, home of that culinary Mecca, 'The Welcome Break'.

A brief search showed him to be innocent and he went on his way. I asked Tara what she was looking for.

'Unmarked vans, hire-cars, lone male drivers,' she explained. Apparently smuggling is still common and a lot of the smugglers are not too bright. Last year, amidst Press reports of cuts to the Customs service, it seems that some amateur smugglers had carrier bags full of cannabis just lying on their back seats as they passed through. 'For a while,' she went on, 'every room in the building had someone detained in it.'

On the other side of the shed, a battered Ford Transit van was being systematically unloaded. Crate after crate of French beer was being piled up on the floor. This was the newest breed of smuggler. Difficult to argue that it was all for personal consumption, especially when these people are known to make the trip two or three times a week. Customs officers are no longer much bothered about the occasional extra bottle of spirits but this was excessive. In addition, the work focuses on drugs, illegal immigrants and arms-smuggling. Tara said that most drug hauls tend to be large and that heroin and amphetamines are as common as cannabis. Tara is clear-minded in her views of the punters.

'We all get a real buzz when we make a bust. The professional smugglers take it calmly but the novices sometimes break down. Sometimes they actually use children as part of their cover. Really upsets us.'

I liked Tara and found her fellow officers I met quite unlike the authoritarian stereotype I had always imagined. Even so, I suspect that my guilty feelings when passing through Customs will remain for a long time.

SANDI Other people's hobbies are always tricky to come to terms with. The obsessive person stands apart, eyeing mere mortals with disdain as they gather the paraphernalia of their preoccupation. Welcome to fishing. Out on the breakwater with escape only possible by boat, the anglers of Dover were preparing to fish through the night.

From a distance, the harbour breakwater appears as a vast concrete dental dam for some sparring giant. Up close it's surprisingly pretty, with large cobblestones making up the narrow walkway. Metal railings run either side to prevent fishermen hurling themselves into the sea and joining their marine friends. Before the fairly recent arrival of the railings, it was not entirely uncommon for an imbibing angler to 'have a few' and tip over the side. It's bad form when your friends have to fish you out instead of two large plaice and a tidy bit of cod.

The Dover Sea Angling Club is one of the richest angling clubs in the country. It's got about 2000 members, perhaps 50 of whom were competing this

evening. It runs a kind of canteen in one of the wartime gun emplacements. In the same arrangement of rooms in which you might reasonably seek a Minotaur, Coke, tea and coffee were for sale beneath calendars of women so large-breasted they could poke your eye out at ten paces. The club chairman has a permanent room behind the canteen. It contained an old army cot, a car-boot sale of ancient fishing equipment and, on a dusty shelf, something formerly living but now either pickled or only partially alive in a jar.

The competition is judged by weight. You can catch what you like and then it's all weighed together. A couple of weeks ago somebody had rather spoiled the event by catching a 25-pound stingray, which is the fishing equivalent of hitting a hole in one. Fishing positions, allocated by a draw, were marked all along the walkway and in each spot an angler was carefully laying out equipment and thermos flasks for the night.

This is no fair-weather hobby. Club members often stay overnight, using the old barrack rooms, and some will even spend two weeks out there in September, concentrating on night fishing. On this fine evening, walking along the breakwater was a pleasure, but I fail to see the appeal of being out there in bad weather, living in spartan conditions with a few maggots for company, when there is a perfectly comfortable large town five minutes away across the water.

There were only two women anglers. One of them, Pat, squatted under a large umbrella, preparing her lines for the night's competition and wearing a smock denoting her membership of the England Ladies team. She enjoys the one-night competitions but in her ten years of angling Pat has had to become hardened to sexist jibes. The men still argue that the women cannot really compete on equal terms but, according to Pat, apart from casting – when a man's strength may give him an advantage – there is no skill exclusive to males. Fishing arouses surprising passion and Pat angrily denounced world fishing competitions, claiming that the men want to banish women from the sport entirely. She recounted a conversation with the Welsh male captain.

'Why don't you have a women's team?' she asked him.

'We don't want anyone to know that it's possible for women to do fishing,' he replied.

We stood chatting as she prepared her lines. Once again I found a stranger offering me intimate thoughts and recollections. She told me of her difficult childhood and present-day problems. I am still surprised that people feel I will understand all their troubles because of what I've been through. It is a great privilege. I just wish I had the answers.

SANDI Further down the walkway, an earnest chap was preparing his bait. He seemed to have so devoted his life to the sport that his face had taken on every aspect and contortion of a bewildered pollack. He had made some attempt at human features in the eyes and nose area but then, as his face progressed downwards, he'd rather given up and the concept of a chin had eluded him entirely. As I contemplated throwing him back, he told me he writes about fishing for a living and fishes in his spare time. I asked what his wife thought about that and he said: 'Well, at the moment she's very busy with the children but once they're grown up and left home she'll have no excuse and she'll have to come fishing with me'. I imagined her imploring her children well into their middle age to stay at home.

He told me there was some trouble last year when the first woman ever to stay on the fortnight break complained about the pictorial array of nude women in the canteen. I asked what happened. 'She learnt she'll just have to put up with it,' said the pollack as he calmly cut up bait on his lap. I eyed the worms. You could clearly see their tiny little mouths going up and down in what must pass as grub distress.

'We have a good laugh,' he went on. 'Sometimes we show blue movies on the wall of the canteen. The fellas go mad running around naked at night.'

My, what fun.

Dover to Hastings

SHIP'S LOG: LIGHT VARIABLE WINDS, SEA STATE CALM.

SANDI Away to Hastings on another fine day. We shall get spoilt at this rate. We marked the point on the GPS for the moment we crossed over the top of the Channel Tunnel. It was a curious thought to be out there on this lovely calm sea in beautiful sunshine while below us engineers were busy finishing the tunnel like demented moles. Tom is rather anti-tunnel.

'I don't think the British wanted the tunnel at all,' he opined. 'I bet as quick as the Frenchmen were digging towards England, the English were filling in the hole. I can't see the point of it. Still, it's always there for somebody to blow up.'

With that cheery thought we passed on.

Later, we saw a boat flying the European ensign, which sent Tom into a rage. He said the blue flag with its circle of European gold stars is not a proper flag and it is illegal for yachts to be dressed in that way. He said that if you have a boat which is registered in Britain, it should be flying the red ensign and any other boat should be flying its national colours. I asked him what I should fly as a Dane.

'The red ensign with a Danish courtesy flag,' he replied.

I asked about Germans, who might not be too popular, sailing into Alderney waters flying the colours of the Fatherland. Tom conceded that perhaps a European flag might be a little more politic. There are so many rules, courtesies and civilities associated with sailing which I'm only just beginning to get the hang of. It seems to me that waving our nationalities in others' faces has caused too much trouble in the past. I like the sense at sea that all sailors are united in their concern for each others' welfare.

The famous white cliffs became small beacons behind us as we smoothed the waters past the grand view of Folkestone. Its elegant buildings are reminiscent of a more sedate time when men in straw boaters strolled along the sea front and did not share their bare bellies with the world.

 As we came abeam of the Dungeness nuclear power plant I was harassed by an enormous bumblebee. Set on a spit of sand dunes, next to a group of old cottages and a lighthouse, the power station looks like one of those huge, secret centres for world domination in the Bond movies of the 1960s and 70s. A huge geyser of water spurted out at the sea a little way from the shore and I wondered whether the aggressive bumblebee was some kind of radioactive, mutant creation.

We seem to be beating fast on this leg of the journey, for Hastings hove into view rather quicker than any of us were anticipating. Perhaps it always feels fast on the homeward stretch.

Hastings's wide beach is littered with colourful fishing boats which lie like giant flotsam and jetsam upon the shingle. Behind them are the tall black fish-drying sheds and a funicular railway rises up steep cliffs into the Sussex countryside. There is no marina so John and I were going to have to make a bit of a D-Day landing via the inflatable. We pumped up the Moby, put on our life-jackets and set to with the oars. The beach was crowded with holiday-makers and we were a strange sight as we arrived wearing an absurd amount of equipment for such a warm day and dragging our boat behind us.

We were a bit stuck once we'd arrived. *Hirta* had to move on and we were due to spend the night at a hotel. John and I wandered into town to look for transport. Hastings was buzzing as we wandered amongst hordes of holiday-makers, past fishmongers and ice-cream vendors along the front. There didn't seem to be any taxis but we spied a chap who was giving horse and buggy rides.

OPPOSITE: *Sandi working the foresails.*

'Could you take us to our hotel?' I enquired.

'Too hot,' he replied. 'Don't want to wear the horse out.'

We stood around for a bit longer.

'Drop you 200 yards away from it,' he offered. 'I'll have to charge more than the normal six quid. Be a tenner.'

There seemed to be no choice so we climbed up into the buggy. It was rather pleasant clip-clopping along the seaside in an open carriage and we were rather cheery when he dropped us off. He pointed us round a corner and departed. In the heat of a hot, noon sun and wearing a ridiculous amount of clothing, John and I nearly expired as we trudged over a mile up a steep hill. If I ever find that man again I will make him walk up, but he'll have to carry the horse.

The Battle of Hastings actually took place 6 miles inland of the town. I bet even in those days there was some bloke with a horse who was willing to take the soldiers up for a price.

DAY 63 Hastings

 A foggy, misty morning again. I went down early to the beach to see the boats coming in. There was an atmosphere of drama as the few fishing boats appeared out of the fog and headed straight for the beach. There is no harbour along this section of coast so the boats have wide, flat sterns to cope with the waves as they sit in the surf waiting to be winched up the beach. Their wide flat bottoms are designed to ease their path across the shingle. Winches dragged the vessels over planks relayed by the crew from the stern to the bow. In the fog it was easy to picture horses in place of the winch engines – it was a timeless scene.

POSTCARD NUMBER 11:
High points of Ye Olde Hastings. Seagulls, churches, and you phone from here.

I spoke to Paul, the skipper of one of the boats. 'My family have been fishing here since the 1600s. There's plenty of other fellas the same,' he explained. 'Local council tried to get rid of the boats to make more room for the tourists. We saw them off.'

I'm glad. At first sight the section of the beach had looked a mess, but after wandering around it for a while I'd begun to appreciate the order of a working environment. Attractive wooden clinker-built vessels were drawn up in a line. Metal winch cables coiled around piles of netting waiting for repair and drying in the sun. The fishing fleet adds greatly to Hastings's charm: the town, like Whitby, presents an honest blend of tourism and the older tradition of fishing with its industrial images.

The council may not need to drive the boats away; the lack of fish is doing that. Paul acknowledged that there has been over-fishing but recent mild winters have caused a new problem. Spider crabs have been over-breeding: 'Every time we bring in the nets they're filled with crabs instead of fish'.

This morning he had only caught three fish: one for him, one for his mate and one for the man who worked the winch. They are all praying for a cold winter to see off the crabs.

I was off to visit a peer and political party vice-chairman. Just my idea of a good time. Lord Tiverton, formerly Derek Howell, gentleman and entrepreneur, is a wealthy man who made millions out of health foods. Down the quiet charm of George Street, at the back of old Hastings with its parades of antique shops, I knocked on Lord Tiverton's door. He opened it sipping a glass of Champagne and commanding me to call him Tivvers. A white-haired gentleman, perhaps in his sixties, he was wearing a pair of spray-on leopardskin leggings, a T-shirt proclaiming the number of votes he received in the last election (282) and an elaborate Cartier copy of a Duchess of Windsor bracelet encrusted with diamonds around two leopard's heads. It's not what you expect from a Lord but then he is vice-chairman of the Monster Raving Loony Party and a complete sweetheart.

I entered his town house and my brain slipped a gear. The narrow hall was painted matt black. Ahead of me, a glass lift with gold trim stood ready to bear us up to the living quarters. Up on the wall the utility meters for the house had been painted in fluorescent colours and framed with an ornate piece of gilt. A golden cot with a doll in it and a small dress on a hanger stood on a ledge while, higher up, another space had been tiled and fitted with a loo and sink which no one would ever be able to get to. The Tantalus of toilets. Sipping bubbly, we ascended.

Tivvers is a man with a zest for life and no time for cooking. We wandered past

OPPOSITE: *Our D-Day landing beach, Hastings.*

LEFT: *Lord Tiverton, vice-chairman of the Monster Raving Loony Party, with his election agent Cherie of Cherie's Clubs for the Unattached.*

the Cynthia Payne Bedroom Suite and into what might once have passed as a kitchen. A microwave, a toaster and a tin-opener, standing on a small square labelled with a felt-tip pen as Kitchen, were the only concessions to cooking devices. Beside them, the single flat surface had a further square foot marked off in felt pen with the word Larder. Stacked into this demarcation were a couple of tins of baked beans and some Sarson's vinegar. Tivvers eats out.

The kitchen was guarded by a life-sized stuffed bear with a dummy in its mouth. The Ursidae creature balefully surveyed the gallery of photographs of Tivvers with the famous. Cynthia Payne, former brothel-keeper and now Chief Whip for the Monster Raving Loony Party, grinned out of most of them. Through large double doors beside a kidney-shaped pool in a large conservatory sat Cherie, Tivvers's business partner and election agent. She also wore a loony T-shirt. Cherie runs clubs for the unattached, aptly named Cherie's Clubs for the Unattached. She gave me a pink envelope and a matching pen with full details of how I could run my own Cherie club. It's certainly a career thought if I don't open that garden centre.

Tivvers put on a black felt top hat with a yellow band on it for the Monster Raving Loony Party and took me for a drive. In a garage carpeted in deep blue was the most immaculate open-top yellow Rolls-Royce and Peter, an immaculate chauffeur in grey uniform. We sank into cream leather seats in the back. Surrounded by polished walnut trim, Tivvers began to tell me his political policies. I think it had all gone to my head because it sounded like the most sensible platforms I had ever heard.

All politicians are crazy but Monster Raving Loony Party people will actually admit it. Tivvers used the European butter mountain as an example. It was absurd that such a thing should exist so the party appointed Eddie the Eagle as their Sports Minister and put forward the suggestion that the butter mountain should be turned into an artificial ski slope. This caused something of an uproar in the papers but

something was eventually done about the matter. I asked Tivvers for his solution to the fishing industry problem in Hastings. 'I think they should extend the English territorial waters to within 100 yards of France. After all,' he asked, 'what have they ever done for us?'

He presented me with a membership form for the party. It included a one million pound bank note bearing a picture of Margaret Thatcher and the words 'I promise the bearer the cheque's in the post'. Apparently, if you join for £7.95, you get a certificate of sanity along with your membership card. I told him the cheque was in the post.

DAY 64 Portsmouth

 We arrived in Portsmouth in great style, sailing up past HMS *Warrior*, the first iron-clad warship, past the latest aircraft carrier HMS *Invincible* and the royal yacht *Britannia* to moor in No. 1 Basin, right under the stern of HMS *Victory*, the flagship of the home fleet. It was extraordinary to come up *Hirta*'s

companionway, past the portrait of Nelson that Tom keeps above his chart table, and walk out on deck to see *Victory*'s magnificent stern rising above me.

~~∞~~

SANDI I visited Portsmouth Sports Injury Clinic. Not your typical tourist trip but they have the technology to rebuild. Wendy Rofe and her assistant basically did an hour and a half's repair job on my hands and arms. The pain has got a lot worse and Wendy gave me some additional splints to wear higher up my arms which have lately gone quite dead. It's a jolly good job that we're on the home stretch because I really don't think that I can do much more.

DAY 65 Portsmouth

JOHN One of *Hirta*'s blocks which had become troublesome way back at the start of the voyage in the Minquiers has given up completely. We've been right round Britain and met no one who could fix it. The captain constructor of the shipyard, who had welcomed us in, said one of his chaps would have a look at it. Portsmouth had once been the biggest block factory in the world. We were in the right place. Deep in the bowels of *Victory*, up near the bow, Tom and I met George Lawrence, one of the carpenters restoring the great ship. He was replacing deck beams that had been damaged during a German bombing raid. The restoration began in 1922 when *Victory* was lying as a hulk. George has worked on her for twenty-five years and is due to retire in 2005, when the restoration should be completed to coincide with the 200th anniversary of the Battle of Trafalgar.

A little man with bright eyes and a ready wit, George spoke movingly of his love for the ship and the bond he feels with all those men who have worked and sailed on her since she was built in the late 1750s. 'We found a note last year in an old beam,' he recalled with excitement. 'Been left there by carpenters working generations ago.' George and his mates had written their own note and hidden it away behind the new beam for a future generation to find.

'Any chance of a hand with this?' asked Tom, holding up *Hirta*'s damaged block.

'Leave it with me and I'll see what I can do,' said George.

We left George working. There was no sense of *Victory* being a museum; although she is a place of profound respect, she is not a shrine but a living entity that continues to inspire visitors as well as those who have the privilege of sharing in work that has gone on for over 200 years.

TRADITIONAL TATTOOS

The practice of tattooing the body is prehistoric, but the word 'tattoo' is comparatively new. It came from Polynesian languages like Tahitian and Samoan and was introduced to England by Captain Cook in 1769. He also brought us the word 'taboo' and helped to prevent scurvy. A lot of modern designs focus on horror objects – skulls and so on. Traditional tattoos were brought back from the West Indies. It was a kind of souvenir for sailors: the physical equivalent of getting a car-sticker or a badge for your walking stick.

At one time, sailors used to have a pair of open eyes tattooed on to their eyelids to warn them of danger. I've seen tattooing done and I'd rather be in danger. Down under the arches of Portsmouth Harbour Station they've been pricking and inking for years. Mr Smith, the tattooist, is a small, quiet man with glasses. Entering his small office was like paying respects to some shady counterfeiter. He sat at a cramped desk surrounded by bottles of ink and discarded rubber gloves. In the small waiting room, two young men idly followed a football game on the telly beneath a virtual wallpaper of potential tattoos.

Mr Smith was intense about his work. While he showed me photos of people whose whole heads or, in some instances, whole bodies were covered in tattoos, I asked him how you decide to take it up as a career. He frowned. 'Well, probably as a child you first see a tattoo, maybe on a relative, and for some people that's just an interest but for others it becomes a way of life.'

Boys still tend to have the word 'Mum' somewhere in their first tattoo so they get into less trouble when they go home. It's only once Mum has calmed down that they move on to line-drawings of girls with unbelievable breasts and occasionally detailed genitalia. Two chaps waiting were both having the Portsmouth Football Club logo tattooed on to their forearms.

'My wife's going to be furious,' said one. 'I don't know. I mean, I took her out all day yesterday.'

'That was kind,' I said.

'Yeah, well, it was her birthday but I mean, if I did that, why can't I have another tattoo?'

He'd already got a sailor with 'Up Pompey' on his arm and sat dabbing at his new engraving with a bit of tissue. He was a mere tattoo trifler compared to Gary.

Gary was a beefcake. He gave the appearance of being able to toss a caber with a Scotsman attached. He was a surprisingly gentle chap who just happened to be

OPPOSITE: *In basin Number 1, Portsmouth. John posing below Nelson's bedroom.*

awash with tattoos. He'd had one arm done in New Zealand and the other done in Australia and a sort of Viking thing on his back. He happily showed me his bottom where a very graphic penis on legs chased the equivalent female bits. If you had to have such a thing this seemed to be the best place for it. At least he never had to look at it. I don't know whether Gary was a MENSA member. He was having the word 'Tattoo' tattooed on his leg and then a drawing of a tattoo machine below it. He asked what colour I wanted it to be for the filming. I said as he was having it for life it was really up to him.

The dye is made in New York and comes in a rainbow of colours. In a mini Lazy Susan like those chutney containers in Indian restaurants, Mr Smith mixed and prepared his colours. A tracing of the pattern was applied to Gary's leg. Then Mr Smith fitted a sterile needle to a machine held together with a rubber band. The machine gave off the same worrying noise you hear at the dentist's. Gary said it didn't hurt but then he didn't look like a man in touch with pain. You have to leave a new tattoo for ten days. 'It has to scab over,' he explained patiently.

The room seemed hot and claustrophobic to me.

A young woman came in. She was a chef from a nearby hotel and she wanted to have a dolphin done on her bottom. Mr Smith never batted an eye.

'Right, drop your shorts and bend over the chair,' he said, turning to get blue ink. I thought our cameraman, Alex, was going to faint, and certainly his eyepiece misted over.

'Don't you want to think about it?' I asked, as her friend giggled outside the door.

'No,' she replied confidently.

POSTCARD NUMBER 12: *Old boats.*

Soon a dolphin was leaping out of the waves on her behind. When he'd finished, Mr Smith stuck a piece of kitchen towel over the tattoo with some Sellotape and told her not to pick at it. Fascinated, I pursued her to the door.

'Won't your parents be cross?'

'Oh, they won't know,' she replied.

I hope they don't watch television.

Mr Smith neatly put away his tools. He said he always tries to talk people out of having names engraved or anything obscene which they might regret. Gary had 'Gary and Maggie' on his arm and I asked if he was still with her. This turned out to be a sore point as Maggie had married someone else last week.

Information had been passed to us from *Victory*: 'Sunset will be at 2058 tonight'. It was so precise that we didn't dare be late. At half past eight we strolled up *Victory*'s gangway to attend the sunset lowering of the ensign.

ON THE FIDDLE

For ease of manufacture and storage, the plates on board HMS *Victory* were square. Food served on them became 'square meals'. The plates had a raised lip, known as a fiddle, around their edges. When a sailor took more than his fair share of food and it slopped over the edge, he was 'on the fiddle'.

Nelson defeated the Danes at Copenhagen so I can't say he's my favourite but he had a nice boat. It's a curious thing approaching her at night, this incredibly orange and black ship fighting the confines of the dry dock. It looks unnatural for her to be so stationary. We walked up a gangplank and entered through a narrow doorway in the side which was so low that even I had to duck my head. The tourists had all gone for the day and the deck was still and silent in relief. Cannons and cannonballs lined the walls and seemed to cast images of the sweat and smell of battle. John and I trod slowly and carefully. It was a unique privilege to walk the worn floorboards alone. The popularity of *Victory* as a tourist attraction means hardly anyone ever gets to see the boat without fighting a crowd.

Down in Nelson's rather luxurious quarters we looked at the narrow swinging cot he slept in. In keeping with tradition, it was a coffin draped to look like a bed but ever-ready for its original purpose. Made me think of Michael Jackson, for some reason. Gleaming brass led us upstairs to the afterdeck. On the main deck a plaque marks the spot where Nelson fell and received a final kiss from Captain Hardy. A strange V-shaped rigging of nets runs across the middle of the deck and along some of the sides. Here the sailors used to roll up their hammocks and store them – neat, and a good protection against snipers in the closely fought battles.

On the afterdeck a bugler in full, spanking, smart uniform was pacing up and down wetting his lips as the commanding officer for the evening stood to attention with an ordinary seaman. The sailor was wearing the tightest suit I've ever seen. His absurdly short flared trousers gave the impression that he had stepped in at the last moment. He stood facing the ensign at the stern with the officer behind him and the bugler to one side. All around us we could see other naval boats waiting for *Victory*'s cue to lower their flags in the official marking of sunset.

I don't know if the young rating had a sneaky watch on him but he seemed to know instinctively when the correct moment came. At 2058 precisely he called out 'Sunset, Sir!'. The officer gave his order in return and as the bugler sounded the end of the day call, the flag was slowly lowered. I don't like the whole notion of military matters and training young people to kill other young people but I confess that even I had a bit of a lump in my throat as the sun sprayed its final colours of the day on to the deck where Nelson fell.

![JOHN] All around, on *Britannia*, on *Invincible* and on other modern warships nearby, we could see the same ceremony being performed as their crews followed the lead of the flagship of the home fleet. It was a very beautiful and moving scene.

![SANDI] Afterwards, our bugler talked about life as a Royal Marine musician. 'There are about 120 different calls to learn,' he explained. 'I'll be honest, I can't see the point of some of them. I mean, a ship goes by and it calls to us and we have to call back. Why?' I thought it was good he wasn't just taking the job lying down.

He spends most of his time on the royal yacht *Britannia* – an incredibly sleek-looking cruising ship which we could just see at the next dock, her dark blue hull standing out against the paler blue waters of Portsmouth Harbour. Not too luxurious for the crew, by all accounts.

'We sleep three to a room in triple bunks with one small locker each,' he said.

'Do you have much to do with the royals?' we asked.

He shook his head. 'Never ever spoken to them. They have lines painted on the deck round the ship to keep us away. Lovely boat. Don't half roll around, though.'

John and I wandered down to have a look. Through the windows we could see the elaborately carved wooden chairs and ornate décor of the dining room. I once spent the night alone on the old British royal yacht. It has been turned into a comedy club in Stockholm. I was a guest and slept in the bed which the Queen

and Prince Philip are supposed to have used on honeymoon. There is talk of scrapping *Britannia*. I'd buy her.

DAY 66 Portsmouth to Lymington

SHIP'S LOG: WINDS NORTH-WEST FORCE 3,
SEA STATE CALM.

JOHN One of George's fellow chippies leant over beneath *Victory*'s stern this morning and handed Tom the renovated block. It was like new. George had sent his best wishes for the rest of our journey and his apologies for not being there in person; he was having a day off at the races.

We moved away from *Victory*, out of No. 1 Basin and out towards the Solent. Before turning west for Lymington we saw *Britannia* coming out behind us. It is a nautical tradition to salute all royal and naval ships by dipping your yacht's ensign. Tom said too many people did it for a lark, yachties rushing to dip their flag in order to make some poor sailor run all the way down to the back of the royal yacht and respond. Anxious to carry out the procedure correctly, he rehearsed me in the etiquette. As *Britannia* came abeam of us, looking magnificent with the masts and funnels of warships lined up behind her, I held the ensign, on its short staff, out over our stern and lowered it slowly. Sailors on *Britannia*'s afterdeck returned the salute and, once her ensign was again flying high, I replaced ours.

I was surprised at how proud I felt. I'm wary of those traditions of ours which seem only to maintain ancient privileges, but seeing *Britannia*'s sleek lines and the impressive precision and courtesy of her crew, I was saddened to think that soon we might all be denied the right to appreciate the great yacht because of yet another cost-cutting exercise.

SANDI Everyone must have heard we were coming. The flight carrier, *Illustrious*, was also on parade in the harbour. Bedecked in flags, the crew celebrated Princess Margaret's arrival to re-dedicate the boat. High above our heads, the flight deck was packed with people in unsuitable summer frocks waiting for a fly-past.

I knew Hawker Harriers are fast. I had no idea they can part your hair as they go past. One just shot past us, with John swearing that he never even got a chance to focus his camera. The pilot must have heard him because he returned to hover right above the deck of the flight carrier. The plane seemed to defy all notions of gravity and sense as it lingered, eyeing the guests and then dipping its nose in salute. We were so close we could actually see the two pilots. In fact, with a decent pair

Harrier jump jet defying gravity over HMS Illustrious *in Portsmouth harbour.*
(Princess Margaret is third from the left on the bridge.)

of binoculars, I venture we could have read their name-tags. Incredibly courageous, these guys. One false move and it would have been a messy business. We could see the Princess and her party on a walkway just below the bridge. It was probably a regular working day for her.

—————— ⌘ ——————

We arrived in Lymington on the eve of Cowes Week and I added another first to my nautical experience; going racing on one of the Solent's top racing yachts, 43-foot *Red Sorcerer*. This greyhound of the yachting world had a new set of sails for Cowes Week and the crew wanted to test them in race conditions. We arrived at *Sorcerer* to find Titch Latchford, the tactician, checking the gear with her team as she waited for the owner's arrival.

'There are normally eleven of us,' she explained, 'but we're down to five tonight. It's going to be busy.'

I went below and found that, apart from a chart table and a one-ring gas cooker, the whole boat was filled with sailbags: not a seat or bunk in sight. It's more a sleek floating sail platform than a yacht. A far cry from *Hirta*.

Five minutes before the race was due to start, a helicopter swooped low over the marina and landed smartly in the car park. Within a minute the owner, Don Woods, had emerged, walked along the pontoon, boarded the yacht, taken his position at the helm and was manoeuvring the boat out to the start line. Hardly a word had been spoken.

As the crew started setting the new sails, Titch gave a countdown to the race start and outlined the course to Don. Standing at the tiller giving orders from behind his blue reflecting sunglasses, he was the epitome of a man used to getting things done. A cool customer.

I tried to follow the crew's movements, but everything happened at once. Two men wrestled with the mainsail as another prepared to hoist the spinnaker, which alone had seven ropes. Ropes were running everywhere and I began tracing them up and down the mast as Pol had taught me. Their ends lay like spaghetti in a tangled mess on the cockpit floor, the only clue to what was what being in a variety of subtle colour codes. Despite the fast action, the atmosphere was calm and controlled. Suddenly the sails were set, a colourful spinnaker gently billowing ahead of us like a giant kite, and the race was underway. We started picking up speed, moving up through the fleet of yachts in the light breeze.

'What's your main concern?' I asked Don.

'Insanity,' he replied briefly.

I was relieved when this turned out to be the name of a rival yacht. As he manoeuvred us away from most of the pack, the film-crew and I did our best to keep out of the way. We avoided the crew, but not the sails. One gybe left Alex, who had just perched himself high on the side to film, pinned behind the massive foresail just inches above the water. We managed to disentangle the equipment, drag it across the boat and pull him out as well. Don and his team were tolerant of our antics and even explained the finer points of racing sail trim and tactics. To be honest I was concentrating so much on hanging on and not getting in the way that the rest went over my head.

It was obvious that our hosts lived for racing and I felt the same enthusiasm bubbling up in me. This was exciting stuff. There was no standing on ceremony. Don ordered me to operate one of the winches, then calmly explained that I had the rope the wrong way round. But at least I'd become part of the crew. The adrenalin was surging as we changed tack and the boat heeled over. We were all ordered on to the higher, weather side to give the boat more stability. We sat there with our legs dangling overboard. Don explained that a fraction of an inch of movement in the hull's position in the water might make the difference between winning and losing.

OPPOSITE: *Crossing the finishing line, Lymington.*

We neared the finish line neck and neck with our main rival, *Insanity*. The light breeze reduced the boats to an agonizingly slow pace, forcing the two skippers into poker-nerved tactics of sailing within feet of each other, trying to take the wind from each other's sails. We finished the race inches ahead. We had been out for an hour and twenty minutes but it seemed like a quarter of an hour to me. I felt the same euphoria I had known after our sail into Stromness and was eager to acquire that still elusive understanding of wind and water.

Don once held the record for the Round Britain Race. He had made our trip in 26 days, 4 minutes and 51 seconds.

We shall soon have been at sea for over two months.

THINGS TO BEAR IN MIND
WHEN PLOTTING A COURSE

1 **The local tidal stream – will it be pushing you forwards or backwards, how fast and at what time?**
2 **The wind. On average, a boat heading in one direction makes between 7 and 10 degrees leeway. That is to say it is pushed off course by about that amount depending on the direction of the wind.**
3 **A calculator is better than an old pencil.**

The state of my hands meant that joining John in the race was out of the question for me. I sat on deck reading Tom's book, *Inshore Navigation*, and trying to get to grips with the whole subject. Tomorrow John and I are to make a passage from Newtown on the Isle of Wight to Lymington, sailing a boat on our own. My hands may be failing me but I am determined to make the correct course on the chart. It isn't simple. You can't just decide that you are at A and that you need to get to B, and plot a line between them. There are lots of other things to bear in mind, such as tidal streams. A tidal stream will push you off your course as soon as look at you. Then there's that infernal wind shoving you about and tides knocking on the door for a bit of a say so.

There is a lot of maths involved. Tide tables are not printed for each area because if they were there'd be so many you'd have to carry them around in wheelbarrows. Instead, the annual almanac prints the tables for a number of standard ports and then gives the variation to be calculated for other harbours in the vicinity. I sat sucking my pencil and thumbing backwards and forwards through tables and tables of calculation. It was a good job nobody wanted a decision in a hurry.

The sun warmed *Hirta*'s decks. In the distance, the billowing spinnakers of the racing boats exploded colour across the horizon. Somewhere out there John and my technical boys were holding on for dear life. I carefully checked the transits I would need to lead us in tomorrow.

NAVIGATING AND PILOTING

Words which separate the amateur from the *cognoscenti*. Navigating is done at sea. Once you get visuals to guide you it becomes pilotage.

THE LYMINGTON RIVER

POSTCARD NUMBER 13: *More boats.*

DAY 67 Lymington to Newtown (round trip)

SHIP'S LOG: WINDS NORTH-WEST FORCE 3 OR 4.

John's and my big day. We went down to the marina early. I checked the navigation charts to make damn sure I wasn't going to hit anything. We'd had enough trouble on the Norfolk Broads. Still, this had to be easier; there were no reeds in the way.

Winter's Gold lacked the grace of *Hirta* and the sophistication of *Red Sorcerer*, but she was ours for the day. A 28-foot sailing boat with mainsail, a large foresail called a genoa and – luxury of luxuries – winches. She's not what you might call a loved vessel. A yacht club flag hanging like a limp tea-towel at the back gave us a clue but I think the real give-away were the cobwebs on the tiller. Tom laughed at the state of her as he boarded to oversee our trip. My hopes of a successful outing were boosted enormously when I actually managed to raise the mainsail without braining Sandi.

As Sandi had found on the Broads, it took me a while to get used to steering with a tiller. But once Tom had reminded me of how to turn the bow closer towards the wind and ease the boat's heeling, I felt far more confident. It was sheer enjoyment seeing how close to the wind I could bring her before the sails started flapping and I had to bear away again. The tiller had an extension, allowing me to stand on the cockpit seat for a better view ahead. With reflector sunglasses like Don's, I could see myself breaking all manner of records. Then the tiller extension came off in my hand.

215

SANDI The engine sounded like something happier in the world of industrial sewing but at least it had a bit of a kick to it and we were able to come out astern from the mooring and putter our way out of the yacht haven. We had a lovely run down towards Newtown, getting to know the boat. Tom tried us on various exercises such as gybing the boat by bringing her stern round through the wind and then giving a little Lambada-style hip-wiggle to steady her on to the new course. Happy that we were doing well, Tom went below into the tiny cabin. At that moment the wind gusted up and the boat heeled right over to such an alarming pitch that I was not at all sure what to do. I pushed the tiller and brought her head to wind. In fact I stopped her completely, but at least I had pushed the boat in the right direction and overcome my Broads-induced fear of the tiller.

When you're actually in charge of a boat, time seems to pass in a flash. We were in Newtown quicker than you could say 'Avast behind' with a straight face. Ahead of us, between the red and green entrance buoys, a classic transit appeared consisting of a Y-shaped post ahead of one with a lollipop-shaped head. Keep the two in line with each other and you can pass safely into the harbour. The importance of this was highlighted by the fact that rather a large French sailing boat on our port side had gone completely aground on the gravel banks.

With John at the bow calling out instructions, and a bit of toing and froing, we picked up a visitor's mooring. John, Tom and I strolled off to the local for lunch. For half an hour we wandered along a true, classic English country lane with the birds singing and the sun shining, to a pretty pub. A piece of grilled sea bass and a pint and you could really see the point of a bit of a sail, a nice walk and a super lunch.

'You're on your own,' said Tom as we set off back to Lymington. Just to be helpful, the wind had completely changed direction. I was so busy checking my course, looking for traffic, wondering about the wind, that when Tom said 'What's uppermost in your mind?' there were any number of responses. 'Have you thought about that buoy?' he continued, motioning towards a green buoy on the port side. No, of course I hadn't. The tide was pushing us closer and closer to it and we were on course to hit it.

JOHN We could see the tide bubbling fiercely around it and after a brief debate decided it would be best to go downtide of the buoy and avoid any chance of being forced on to it. We tacked successfully and continued safely on our way. Although our manoeuvres were late, slow and clumsy we felt a tremendous sense of achievement in at last being able to judge how we were doing and what we should do next. It was all beginning to make sense. I realized I was doing things that until now had remained skills I admired in others. Tom left us pretty much to our own devices, giving us the chance to spot potential problems and work out how to avoid them, only giving orders if we were really wide of the mark. This was the ideal way to combine what we could do already with information that, though stored at the backs of our minds, had remained untested.

SANDI We were almost triumphant arriving in Lymington and even managed a couple of nifty gybes in the harbour before terrifyingly docking alongside *Hirta*. I'd rather have rammed the *QE2*. I felt we had learnt more in one afternoon than in weeks at sea. I am a big fan of winches.

DAY 68 Lymington to Weymouth

JOHN Sailed to Weymouth past the Needles today and along the Costa del Dorset, as the Cunliffes call it. Felt feverish and out of sorts; possibly heat-stroke from the sail yesterday combined with general exhaustion. But we must press on, we have to be in Falmouth in six days. Getting closer and closer to the end.

SANDI Weymouth is British seaside culture in aspic. Along the front, every house in the town seems to have been turned into a hotel of dubious quality. The beach was packed with people in the way you only ever see in Pathé news-reels. Here was the stuff – Punch and Judy, helter-skelter, donkey rides, a sand sculptor and at the far end the only concession to the 1990s – some fairly fierce volleyball. Everywhere chip-fed men with their shirts off displayed their bellies like prizes. I beat Ros and Hannah in the pedalo race. It was good to find a vessel which suited me even if I did come quite close to taking out several small children on my way to victory.

I was off to assist Professor Guy Higgins with his Punch and Judy show on the beach. I've scaled some showbiz heights on this trip. Guy's a member of the Guild of Punch and Judy Showmen. I can't imagine it's a very big guild. If it had a national conference it could probably have it at my house. On the best beach pitch around Guy gives his Punch and Judy twice a day all through the summer.

Inside his striped, phone-booth-sized 'theatre', all the puppets and props were hanging upside down, ready for Guy to plunge his arm in and bring them to life. He stood on a raised platform and glanced through two gauze windows cut into a backcloth. Everything was most professional. The music went on at the quarter and he made various miked announcements to the audience while two women colleagues collected the 50-pence pieces.

My job was to hand up the sausages. We went through it several times. I don't normally do props. The audience gathered and, after some contretemps with a family who wouldn't pay, we began. It's odd from backstage. You don't get any sense of the plot. Maybe there isn't one. Guy sweated and puffed as Punch worked his way through a traditional medley of wife-beating and child abuse. Guy's very keen on tradition and scathing about the summer amateurs who put on puppet shows. He's appeared with Mr Blobby so I guess he ought to know.

WEYMOUTH

POSTCARD NUMBER 14: *Happy holidaymakers.*

Further along the beach we tried the helter-skelter and looked at a huge model of the *Cutty Sark* made out of sand. The donkeys, in four rows of five, were led by a series of disconsolate-looking young people. They walked the same track backwards and forwards, and backwards and forwards again, with not one single child jockey smiling. Red-faced fathers rushed about getting different angles with camcorders. I don't know who was supposed to be having the good time.

Weymouth is an uneasy alliance between two entirely different towns. There's the rather tacky seafront with its energetic volleyball and then there is the old harbour with its rather smart restaurants and shops set in colourful terraces along the quayside. We ate at Perry's – the best restaurant since Rick Stein's in Padstow. Pale blue walls, lovely calm atmosphere and the most fabulous fresh fish. Wonderful.

Overall, apart from Perry's, we met rather a lot of grumpy people in Weymouth. There's a plaque up at the old harbour which says that it was through Weymouth in the middle of the fourteenth century that the Black Plague first entered Britain and wiped out between one-third and half of the total population. Maybe some of the temper is a relic left over from having had such a horrid time.

DAY 69 Weymouth

 On the Isle of Portland a grim building stands in stark contrast to the seaside fun. The Portland Young Offenders' Institution. Some time ago I was invited to meet some of the inmates in the institute. Throughout our sail round Britain I'd been looking ahead to my visit with a mix of dread and intense curiosity. I had wondered how I would react on re-entering the world of captivity, half-fearing that I would be overcome by memories and break down, yet wanting to see if I had put those years behind me. As we drove in through the double gates I remembered how I had entered Lebanon of my own free will and how the right to leave in the same manner had been denied me. I was, unreasonably, afraid that it might happen again.

Chris Daniels, the resident psychologist, took me first to see the segregation unit where the prisoners or trainees, as the young inmates are called, are sent for violating prison regulations. The cells vary in bleakness depending on the trainee's offence. The worst cases, those who are violent, are put in an empty cell, with bare concrete walls and floor, until they calm down. I felt a horrid fascination for this place; it was so like the rooms I had been held hostage in. I attempted to show some bravado.

'This is what it's all about,' I said flippantly and immediately felt ashamed of my effort to conceal my dread. I knew the torment of being shut in a place such as this; the utter dejection of being reviled by your fellow man and locked away as an animal. I could not bring myself to touch the door; the idea of it closing on someone filled me with horror.

The cell block, where I was to meet two inmates, was exactly what I had imagined; a massive Victorian building with tiers of cells set around a central open space with a safety net across the first level. I was concerned suddenly that I was being voyeuristic without due consideration of my motives and responsibilities. When I met Lee and Paul my fears subsided. We immediately found similarities in our experiences of captivity: worrying about the family at home; coping with the tedium of prison life. They shared the mournful delight in hearing the door banging shut at night with its promise of a few hours' privacy. We talked about the need to find private space and to make the cell as homely as possible: I teased them that Paul's cell where we sat would have seemed like the Ritz to Keenan and me. But there were differences. I was locked away for political reasons, my captors had nothing against me personally, an interest only in my passport and the government

which had issued it. Lee and Paul were held here with the sanction of their own countrymen.

Lee's story was simple. After more than a year of living quietly with his girlfriend and working as an apprentice bricklayer he had gone out for the night with some old friends. At the end of the evening they had got into a fight with some sailors, one of whom was badly injured. Lee had been found guilty of aggravated assault and sentenced to three years' imprisonment. He hoped to be released, on parole, within a year and was very positive that he would not be in trouble again. He had studied for GCSEs and wanted to finish his apprenticeship before trying anything new. Above all, he wanted to resume the relationship with his girlfriend.

Paul's story was more complicated. He has been convicted of a terrible crime, and I can only base my reactions on what I heard from him. He is still fighting to prove what he affirms is his innocence of the conviction for rape for which he and a co-defendant received a seven-year sentence. His co-defendant staged hunger strikes in an effort to gain an appeal hearing. Now he had been transferred to the higher security prison at Dartmoor. Paul told me that they were still trying to get their case reviewed and he had written to the Home Secretary and even the Queen. So far to no avail. Rape carries the same stigma in prison as it does in the outside world but Paul says he is determined to clear his name and air his anger and frustration, even if doing so leaves him open to abuse. He has been faced with the appalling dilemma of forgoing the possibility of parole because, to be eligible, he would have to acknowledge due remorse for the rape. To do that would be the same as confessing to the crime.

His faith in himself is strong and his self-possession impressive. He will need that focus now that he is twenty-two, the upper age limit for trainees at Portland, and will soon have to transfer to an adult prison. His determination to force himself into a position where he will have to see his full sentence out is the strongest argument he could ever make for himself.

What surprised me about these young men was the maturity with which they spoke about their situation and looked forward to the future They were not worldly-wise – indeed, at moments their vulnerability came through clearly – but they were making the best of their captivity. They had taken advantage of the counselling offered by Chris Daniels. Paul, as a member of the Samaritans' prison service, was helping fellow trainees come to terms with jail, themselves and each other. I was impressed by their sense of responsibility, to themselves and their community and to the people they had left at home.

We chatted for a while before Lee had to go back to his block. I said goodbye to Paul and followed my colleagues down the many flights of stairs to the exit. The sound of Paul's door slamming shut stopped me in my tracks. For a moment I was back in Beirut with my heart pounding as I waited for the guards; wondering what was happening outside the cell and whether it would affect me. For those seconds I shrank back into the grey, emotional tyranny of captivity. I did not relax until we were out of the prison completely. The departure through the gates seemed to take an age. Once outside I stood on the cliff and, breathing deeply, looked down at the sea that had become the reality of my former dreams of freedom.

SANDI The Royal National Lifeboat Institute is a splendid institution. If you get into trouble it comes and gets you and you don't have to pay a penny. The whole of the RNLI is supported voluntarily, so of course you have to do what you can. John and I had been asked months ago if we would draw the quarterly lottery. The unbelievable thing was that we were in the right town on the right day to do it. A man with a van had brought the large ticket-drum from HQ in Poole to the Weymouth quayside opposite *Hirta*'s mooring.

An old lifeboat man called Don, wearing his lifeboat shirt and a medal, rowed over in a wooden rowing boat called *The Last Ope* and took us across. Quite a crowd had gathered on the other side of the steps, so we suffered the embarrassment of being applauded up the steps. It is always a moment when you suspect you have dinner down your front. Everyone wants to touch John when he passes through a crowd. We stood in front of a board which declared him Former Beirut Hostage in large letters. I think he will soon prefer Excellent Sailor and Fine Maker of TV Programmes. I drew the first ticket and the two thousand pounds were won by a Mrs Bloggs, which pleased all the RNLI folk. Apparently Bloggs is a famous lifeboat name. I didn't like to ask whether that was for a boat or for someone from a lifeboat family.

JOHN I found it hard to concentrate on drawing winning raffle tickets. I'd moved from the deprivation of prison to the wide, warm spaces of celebrity in a matter of minutes, much as I'd done on coming home from Lebanon. It left me totally disorientated.

SANDI Because of the strong tides, you have to get round Portland Bill at a certain time so *Hirta* had set sail ahead of us. With an accompanying party in unsuitably smart frocks, we set off in the lifeboat to catch up with her. The Weymouth lifeboat is so modern that it can flip over. I wouldn't want it to and in fact neither did the coxswain particularly. He said he couldn't imagine a sea that could actually turn you upside down and leave you there – it would always turn you

back the other way. I wanted to believe him but he also told me that the best thing in the world when you've been out on a shout is corned beef and crackers.

The boat has a capacity of 150 people but it's not that big and I would imagine it would have a bit of a sardine-cruise feel about it with that many on board. John and I took turns steering, doing 18 knots, three times *Hirta*'s fastest speed, as if we were ambling along. We sat in front of an array of the latest equipment – plotting devices, radar and my favourite, a direction-finder which, if the lifeboat makes radio contact with a yacht, automatically plots the vessel's bearing. This saves time. In the old days it was quite common to check out a series of boats before you found the one in trouble.

Then the lifeboat got called out. This is the sort of thing you watch on TV and think 'Oh, they must have set that up,' but we were on a shout and we weren't expecting it. Our producer, Jeremy, began pinging up and down with the excitement of a demented bungee-jumper. A woman had phoned the coastguard to say she'd seen a blue and yellow dinghy floating along and would we check it out. We turned around and headed back. We stopped and checked some water-skiers. Must have been a strange sight for them. A giant RNLI boat steaming towards them with a film-crew, several ladies in printed cottons, a former Beirut hostage and a producer overcome by the thrill of it all. They said they were fine. It's exactly what I would have claimed.

We steamed around for some time and found nothing. The coastguard stood us down. By the time we'd finished the shout *Hirta* was some considerable distance away from us. As we steamed after her John and I stood on the bridge chatting with the coxswain.

'How many lives has this particular boat saved?' I asked, squinting into the rapidly setting sun.

'Impossible to say,' answered the coxswain. 'We never look at it that way. We've never lost anybody and that's the important thing.'

JOHN I stood on the bridge as we sped at 18 knots towards Portland Bill, enjoying the early evening sunshine. I looked up at the cliffs and saw the grim blocks of the Portland Institution silhouetted above them. Free, and realizing a long-held dream, I hoped that once Lee and Paul were at liberty they too would find such fulfilment.

SANDI As we approached *Hirta* we were instructed that we were to climb over the railings of the lifeboat rather than through a wire 'gate' where we've done transfers before. It was extremely tricky and, at the moment when we very nearly lost Jeremy down between the boats, there was a great cracking sound as the lifeboat appeared to ram *Hirta*.

Tom began bellowing: 'Damage! Damage! Damage!' The lifeboat men didn't seem to be that bothered. They thought the noise had come from two fenders making contact and sailed off, waving goodbye. Tom was inconsolable.

'I'll never call you out if I'm in trouble,' he shouted after them. Be quite something to have come this far and be sunk by a lifeboat.

That night, Ros prepared pancakes and being heeled over in the small galley area really tested our skill at tossing them. There were no serious mishaps – those of us who had started this voyage as novices had definitely found our sea-legs.

Our final night passage and my back doesn't mind a bit. That pipe cot is the pits. Along past Portland we could see the great massive blocks of stone which at one time old Sir Christopher Wren sent Thames barges to collect so he could rebuild London. Bloody long way to go to get a bit of stone. You can still see the cranes on the water's edge and up on the cliff tops; hundreds of tiny beach huts in a child's paint-box display of colour.

The weather stayed fine after sunset with a good breeze pushing us along at 5 or 6 knots. Sandi and I stood the first watch and were far more relaxed than on previous occasions. We could see land off to starboard and had a good view of other vessels further out to sea. As Sandi was preparing tea for the next watch I heard the foresails flapping a little and decided to sheet them in. Foolishly I did this on my own and lost control of the helm. *Hirta* came to a full stop. Sandi reappeared and I asked her to summon Tom. He was on deck in seconds, having been woken by the change in motion. He waved my explanations aside, saying: 'It's all right, you just got yourself headed'.

I had let the bow swing right into the eye of the wind and unintentionally had stopped us. Tom explained that we would have to go slowly round in a full circle and then start off again.

I had half-expected him to be angry, but he was not at all put out. His only concern was that I should understand what had happened and remember how to get the boat back underway. Normally such an embarrassing mistake would have left me feeling useless and humiliated but tonight, although angry with myself for not thinking clearly, I focused on the knowledge I had gained as a result.

OVERLEAF: *Under sail.*

DAY 70 On passage to Dartmouth

SANDI After our watch, I slept for about an hour and a half on deck but by 1 a.m. the wind had come up and spray was lashing my face. You could hear everybody below rolling around as we battled with some of the roughest waters yet. The wind was really giving us a buffeting. Below decks *Hirta*'s boards creaked and groaned in protest as she dipped and plunged forward. The blocks on the deck rattled and crashed as we went from one tack to another. The strong head wind made tacking the only way forward and people adopted strange techniques to stay in their bunks. You could see them wedge their bums against a bit of the bed on the low side of the heeling boat. As they lolled off, the boat would come round on to the other tack and they'd find themselves on the high side. There would be a chorus of gasps as everyone shot across the slippery leatherette cover of their berth and banged into the other wall. I gave up.

JOHN Conditions deteriorated steadily. The sea became rougher and rougher and at two o'clock I gave up any hope of sleeping and went up on deck. Tom and Ros were on watch and explained that the wind had come round so much that we would have to beat to windward, tacking all the rest of the way to Dartmouth.

For a short while I found the stormy ride thrilling but soon the unpredictable motion had me sitting forlornly in the cockpit, looking at the friendly lights of Torquay and Paignton ahead and cursing fate for bringing this vile sea between us; we might as well have been a million miles away as we tacked back and forth, never seeming to get any nearer.

SANDI At about 4 a.m. we were passing Brixham. Ahead of us we could see the Start Point lighthouse. Suddenly on our starboard side we saw what appeared to be a light flash. It was quite high up and slightly orangey. We kept looking in the same direction and saw it reappear twice more. There was some discussion about what it meant as Tom said it was the wrong colour for a distress flare. Mindful of our conversation with the RNLI when we were told that the cutbacks in the coastguard service mean the general public must now be the ears and eyes of safety along the British coast, Tom called in the sighting. The coastguards were grateful for the thought but the flares were their own. They said they'd got a rescue craft out searching for a missing woman and they were sending flares off to illuminate the area to try to find her. It was a shock to realize that there could be danger so close to land.

JOHN By dawn I was feeling so bad that I could not decide whom I hated most. I sat outside the cockpit with my knees drawn up under my chin, smoking cigarettes furiously and plotting unspeakable punishments for the first person to ask me to do anything. Everyone was relaxing as the sea calmed and the sun started lighting the land ahead. I could not share in their contentment. Tom and Ros discussed the boat's performance and ideas on how to make her passage easier. I found their talk reassuring but was amazed that they had suffered conditions like this right across the Atlantic. I doubted I would have the stamina for that and would most likely turn about and run for home.

SANDI No one had had any real sleep. John was the tiredest I've ever seen him and fed up. He sat huddled against the companionway on deck, with his cap pulled down low over his eyes, smoking, busy building an exclusion zone around himself against any involvement in anything. He made himself as small and as irritable as possible and we left him to it. Everyone felt the same. We had really had more than enough.

Dartmouth, like some tantalizing mirage, seemed to constantly recede into the distance rather than get any closer. Through the night we had been comforted by the lights of Sidmouth, Teignmouth and Torquay as we crossed Lyme Bay. Now everything was grey and unwelcoming. Dartmouth was much narrower an approach than I'd expected. We strained our eyes for the red and green buoys as we approached the protected harbour with castellations on both sides. It was as if Mother Nature knew we had reached a serious low point: suddenly the harbour opened out and we were presented with a magnificent sunrise over the multi-coloured buildings along the quay.

Despite myself, I could not help but look about as we entered the narrow Dart estuary with its steep cliffs lined with woods and eccentric houses. We went up past Dartmouth and moored at Dittisham, a pretty place, and a comforting distance from the sea.

 It has been an incredibly long haul. Everyone is extremely tired now from constantly being on the move, the incessant travelling, seeing endless new places and people. My arms have really had it. I have incredible pins and needles throughout the top half of my body and pain in my back. We can't describe or enjoy anything new any more. It is time for us to finish. John said he was feeling so fed up when he arrived in Dartmouth that he was cross with himself for ever having enjoyed the journey. I think the last eight- to ten-hour trip to Fowey is going to be a testing time, just to see who gets through it in a good temper.

DAY 71 River Dart

 A day on the mooring on the River Dart. It's very pretty. We've got beyond pretty. I don't even know where I've put my camera.

DAY 72 Dartmouth to Fowey

SHIP'S LOG: WINDS NORTHERLY FORCE 4 OR 5.

Fog was forecast for this morning, threatening, even at this late stage, that we might not make it to Falmouth on time. However, there was only a light haze when we set off down the Dart, past its myriad small creeks as we headed for Fowey. The Dart Valley Steam Railway puffed along, helping to revive my spirits which were already on the mend after a good rest yesterday. I was sorry not to have more time to stop and explore. I made a silent promise to return.

I think it's August now but I wouldn't want to testify to it in court. We're at sea. We're all at sea. We all wish we weren't. The sea is a steely grey and stands out sharply against the white sky with its black clouds, ready and soaked with rain. We've already been drenched once. I went below to dry, came up, thought it

had cleared and now the rain's come down again. I wonder if a person can get so damp that the balance of their body fluids goes? We can see no land whatsoever as we make our journey from … Oh, God, where have we been? Dartmouth, John says it's Dartmouth, round Start Point and along to Fowey where we are due to de-slime the bottom of the boat.

It has been a very billowy journey with absolutely nothing to see and monsoons of rain that even Noah would have rebelled at. Sleeping-sickness has consumed the crew. Jeremy and I prepared a special breakfast as a treat for Ros but she was asleep by the time it was ready. Conversation has become reduced to basic grunts: 'Does anybody want tea?' and 'Who's left this here?' We've got all the sails up in a useless display of optimism. The wind's 'right up our chuff', as Tom likes to say, and doing us no good at all.

DAY 73 Fowey

SANDI Fowey. This is where *Hirta* was originally built eighty-three years ago and so in a sense she's come home. It is a lovely, very Cornish town with incredibly narrow and steep streets which would laugh at any American car. It is all very Daphne du Maurier.

At 4 a.m. *Hirta* was moved to a slipway off the main harbour and tied securely against a wall while we waited for the tide to recede. Throughout the hundreds of miles we have travelled, her bottom has collected slime. I know how she feels. This needs to be wet-wiped off if we are to have any chance of success in the forthcoming classic boat races.

JOHN I have become so familiar with the fact that *Hirta* draws 8 feet of water that it was something of a shock to see her denuded of sea and standing on the dry bed. She is huge. Below the smart black paint, which stands above the water-line, was a rather shockingly pink bottom and a huge keel. I couldn't take my eyes off the rudder. It's all very well turning the wheel hither and thither when you're actually sailing, but there was this enormous piece of wood that actually steers her and a surprisingly small propeller.

We donned full oilskins and set to work scrubbing the hull. Most of the green slime came off with a good rub with sponge and water. Standing on the dock floor, *Hirta* towered above us. No wonder she feels so solid in the water.

SANDI Further up the slipway, the *Atlantic Bay*, a large cargo vessel, was being welded and painted. I hoped she had been tied up securely. One false move and *Hirta* would be matchsticks. Tom began repairing the joins in *Hirta*'s hull. Here's some information I'm glad I didn't have earlier. The planks are held together and prevented from leaking by bits of string bashed in with some putty. This does not sound sufficient to me but Tom exuded confidence. He also exuded speed. The tide had turned and was sploshing back in around us. Whatever work needed doing needed doing in a hurry. I was dispatched to collect some lead putty from the very boatyard where *Hirta* first began life.

Slithering across the slimy slipway, I raced to the yard in a crackle of sweaty oilskin dungarees. Bits of boats abounded as I crossed piles of discarded wood and metal. Here and there, men were working on vessels which seemed beyond repair and nowhere could I spy any gleaming new craft under construction. Up some metal stairs I entered the supply store and stepped back in time. A long counter stood in front of an array of small drawers and shelves bearing mysteries. A young woman nodded when I asked for lead putty and presented me with a piece of torn cardboard bearing a pile of red lead powder and a small mound of white putty. 'Just mix,' she said as if I looked the lead putty type and would know what to do. 'How much is it?' I asked. 'Oh, that's all right,' she said in a comrade sailor sort of way.

It's not easy running with lead powder. I can't imagine it's very healthy to inhale so I loped along shielding the stuff from the wind whilst not breathing. Arriving with my charge intact and gulping like a beached gefilte fish, I handed it to Tom who immediately spilled most of it down his front.

Hirta was patched, the tide came in, tomorrow we race.

DAY 74 # Fowey to Falmouth

SHIP'S LOG: WINDS LIGHT AND VARIABLE,
SEA STATE CALM.

JOHN During the night a number of old boats had gathered in Fowey. Now they were decorating their decks with signal flags and preparing for the 'feeder' race to Falmouth. It seemed a fitting tribute to *Hirta*, having brought us safely right round Great Britain, to race from her home port in the company of lovely vessels of her own vintage.

PREVIOUS PAGE: *Classic boats starting the race from Fowey to Falmouth.*

The word 'race' suggests some kind of urgency to me but this does not apply to classic boats. The start was delayed for no discernible reason and we finally departed without me being aware that the race had started. The wind had dropped and we progressed slower than a snail on a hot tarmac road. Both John and I had been keyed up for the event. Now Hannah slept by the cockpit and most of us strained our eyes for Falmouth.

The small stretch of sea between Fowey and Gribbin Head was covered with a patchwork of sails as gentlemen's yachts from the turn of the century took on classic working boats like *Hirta*. The wind was so light that the fleet just drifted along gently, barely making way. We'd come all the way round the country on time only to be virtually becalmed within sight of our final destination. The race was declared over just before Dodman Point and the engines were turned on.

As we neared Falmouth an old fishing boat came out to welcome us. It had a jazz band on board, which was eccentric, but the jolly Dixieland rhythms echoed our excitement as we neared the end of our great journey.

All hands given permission to celebrate circumnavigation of Britain
(accompanied by jazz band).

Looking for our finish line.

SANDI   I'm not a jazz buff but I have rarely seen or heard a more splendid thing. It is surreal to hear the strains of 'When the Saints Come Marching In' drifting across the open waters. I was surprised to find tears in my eyes. It was so strange to arrive somewhere familiar. We knew this harbour. We had been here before. We even knew other people. I waved to anyone I'd met before as if we were actually related. I blew kisses to the jazz band with whom I was entirely unfamiliar. I wondered if it was only the Pope who was permitted to kiss the ground on arrival. On the foredeck, John and I danced and laughed. We had done it, we had really done it. We had sailed around the coast of Britain and arrived back pretty much in one piece and on time to the day.

JOHN   We all felt a great sense of relief and release and toasted our success with champagne. It seemed a lifetime ago that we had set off from here; we had seen so much and, although it was hard to focus on all the places and people we had visited, we were filled with a great sense of achievement – we had circum-navigated Britain and were home on time. As we entered the main harbour Mike and Tina Rangecroft came out in a boat with Pol. Tina handed over the bottle of

A touch of celebration.

Liberation rum to Sandi, who promptly did the decent thing and we drank another toast, to the Falmouth Classics, *Hirta* and ourselves.

 ## DAY 75 Falmouth

SANDI Everyone was demob-happy. I fully expected Jeremy to hand me a second-hand suit, a fiver and a train ticket home, but first there was one more race to be completed. By now John and I were old race hands. Pol had rejoined the team and we were calm about the race ahead. So was the wind. The harbour was bumper to bumper with old vessels as everyone set sail early to smooch around and show off.

JOHN The great race was more of a long start. We sailed back and forth across the Fal estuary as boats in other classes got started. There was a dreamlike, slow-motion quality to the afternoon as the magnificent old sailing boats tacked back and

ABOVE: Hirta *in
Classics race.*

OPPOSITE: *Touched
by celebration.*

RIGHT: *The hard graft
of intense competition.*

*Entry number 007. Basildon,
Premium and Brooke Bond.*

It's over!

forth, often within inches of each other, barely making any forward progress.
Though it would have been greater fun to be racing with some decent wind, we
did get ample opportunity to admire the opposition.

Tom expertly nipped this large old lady in and out of his competitors,
calling out ribald remarks to everyone he passed. The sky had conceded to
blue and it was a magnificent display of stately seamanship. A folk band strummed
on board an old barge as three gentlemen in tuxedos waved from their small craft.
It was a party and nobody much cared who actually won or lost. There were some

half-hearted moves to outsmart vessels in our class but there was never any real race involved. We sailed and sipped beer and marvelled at where we had been.

JOHN In the evening, the prize-giving in the marquee echoed the casual atmosphere of the racing. Nearly everyone got prizes, but in a spirit of fun rather than competition. What mattered was the pleasure of seeing so many old boats still sailing and their traditions being maintained.

SANDI We swapped sailing anecdotes and clapped people on the back. For one brief night we were true sailors who had circumnavigated Britain.

Final Thoughts

JOHN At the outset of this journey I had hoped to find the 'greed is good' mentality absent. This hope was fulfilled. For so many of the communities we had visited there simply wasn't room for it, indeed it had left those on the edges of British life with little more than a desperate struggle to survive. Yet we had not met a defeated people but one determined to work in unity to find a way out of financial difficulties without losing sight of the value of maintaining a spirit of community. Westminster is too distant and all but irrelevant, its actions failing to take any notice of local needs and aspirations.

Although now physically joined to Europe by the Channel Tunnel, the trends in Europe that seem most relevant to Britain in the mid-1990s are those that look for smaller communities and decentralized government. We have become an island of islands. I believe this can be a positive move, as the spirit driving these communities is one that seeks richness rather than riches and places social responsibility before personal fulfilment.

Sailing had excelled my naive dreams of it. There had been all the pleasure I had imagined but I had gained much more from its difficulties than I had anticipated. The natural frustrations of tides and weather had finally become tolerable because they present everyone with the same problems but also the same opportunities. That is all that the people we had met wanted for their lives. They accept the vagaries of their existence, but want the right to control their own destiny.

SANDI We have travelled so far and so fast that it is difficult to sit back and gain perspective. The variety of landscape and way of life in Britain is so vast that it has surprised us all. No docker in Liverpool can imagine the life of a crofter on

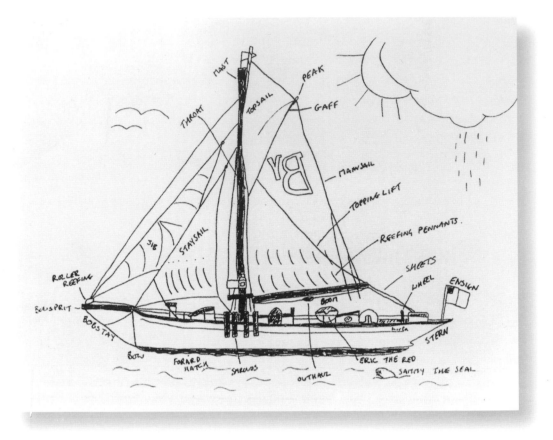

Eigg and no one on Eigg bears any relation to the smart yachties of Lymington. We had been troubled by a pervading air of depression amongst the working people we came into contact with. The industries which sustained the coastal communities of the past are on the wane and there is nothing yet to replace them. As Britain increasingly takes her place in Europe it is the small communities which are in danger of being lost. Yet amongst the doleful murmurings we found such kindness and generosity of spirit that it buoyed us all on the long journey.

In Britain's last year as an island, before the opening of the Channel Tunnel, we did not come across one person who favoured this physical link with the Continent. I'm sure such people exist but I do not think they live by the sea. For those who live within the sight and temper of the seas, Britain is and always will be an island.

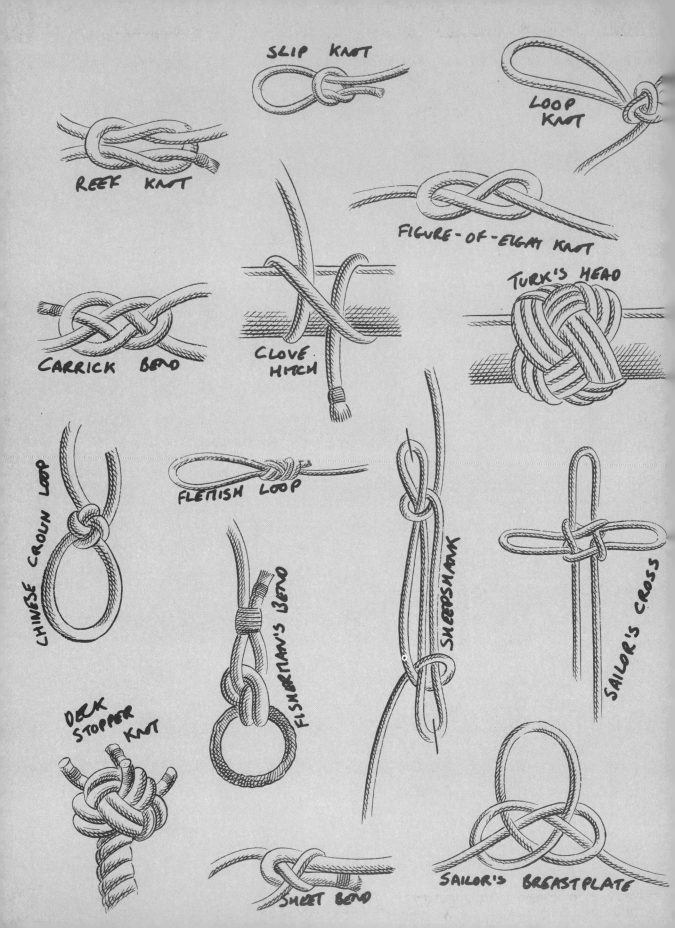

SLIP KNOT

LOOP KNOT

REEF KNOT

FIGURE-OF-EIGHT KNOT

CARRICK BEND

CLOVE HITCH

TURK'S HEAD

CHINESE CROWN LOOP

FLEMISH LOOP

SHEEPSHANK

SAILOR'S CROSS

OAK STOPPER KNOT

FISHERMAN'S BEND

SHEET BEND

SAILOR'S BREASTPLATE